The Best of Everything According to the Numbers

Written by
Michael Robbins

Conceived and Designed by
David Kaestle

WORKMAN PUBLISHING
New York

Produced by
David Kaestle, Inc.

Written by
Michael Robbins

Conceived and Designed by
David Kaestle

Edited by
David Kaestle and
Michael Robbins

Editor for
Workman Publishing
Sally Kovalchick

Data and Information Research
Robert Frenay

Picture Research
Louisa Grassi

Production
Our Designs, Inc.

Associate Art Director
and Graphics Design
David Vogler

Original Photography
Christie Sherman

Additional Research
Catherine Taylor
David Levine
Paul Kaestle

Design and Production Assistant
Daniel O'Brien

Special Thanks
Nat Adriani, Eddie, Jennifer and Daniele Casazza, Mavis Clark, Judy Fireman, Albert Gottesman, Joe and Pauline Grassi, Mike Gross, Gary Ink, Michael Kaestle, Howard Litwak, Wendy Palitz Robbins, Paul Rosenthal, Lynn Strong, David Wilson and, of course, Peter Workman

Extra Special Thanks
We are greatful to the hundreds of helpful men and women, representing our vast number of information and picture sources, who gave us their valuable time and cooperation in assembling the information and pictures presented here. *Top 10* would not be possible without them.

This book is dedicated to David Joseph Kaestle and Patrick William Robbins. Both would make the "Best Kids" chart.

Copyright © 1991 by David Kaestle
All rights reserved.
No portion of this book may be reproduced–mechanically, electronically, or by any other means, including photocopying–without written permission of the publisher.

Library of Congress Cataloging-in-Publication Data
Robbins, Michael W.
    Top 10: the best of everything according to the numbers/by Michael Robbins.
p. cm.
Includes index.
ISBN 0-89480-854-0
1. Curiosities and wonders.   2. World records   I. Title.
AG243.R53 1991
031.01-dc20   90-50370
                                                                                       CIP

Published by
Workman Publishing
708 Broadway
New York, NY 10003

Printed in the United States of America

First printing March 1991

10 9 8 7 6 5 4 3 2 1

INTRODUCTION

Americans love numbers. Numbers carry themselves with an air of surety, of hard realism—as capable of finishing an argument as starting one.

Many of the most telling facts about American popular culture in 1990 or any other year are best expressed in numbers: when you see that *Ghost* was the top-grossing film of 1990, that *Modern Maturity* was the top-selling magazine, that *Roseanne* was the most popular television show, or that Vladimir Horowitz had the top *three* best-selling classical albums, you've learned something—and something rather complicated— about what is happening now in America.

When you know the top 10 in many areas, you pretty much know the score. The top 10 movies, for instance, earn more at the box office than do the next three dozen movies put together. The 10 best-selling toys capture the lion's share of total U.S. sales. And some of the top 10 American corporations control more assets than do many of the world's nations.

But the hits and the numbers change. That's why we're doing *Top 10* as an annual almanac. Every year there is a new crop of movies, records and books. The peak television show of this past season can drop to the valley floor next year. So look for us in 1992 to see who emerges as the superstars, to spot the trends and to learn who's got real staying power and who folds in the stretch.

To support these lists of the year's superlatives, we've included—below the line—the most illuminating anecdotes, annual awards, profiles, all-time greats, astonishing factoids and telling trends in American popular culture for 1990.

CONTENTS

THE CHARTS

 Music

Best-Selling Pop Albums – *11*
Best-Selling Rhythm & Blues Albums – *12*
Top Rap Singles – *12*
Best-Selling Jazz Albums – *13*
Best-Selling Country Albums – *13*
Best-Selling Music Videos – *14*
Top-Grossing Concert Tours – *14*
1990 Grammy Award Selections – *14*
Top Pop Artists – *15*
Best-Selling Classical Albums – *15*

 Movies

Top-Grossing Feature Films – *16*
Top-Grossing Films of All Time – *16*
Studio Market Shares – *17*
Highest-Paid Actors & Actresses – *17*
Top-Grossing Foreign Films in America – *18*
Highest-Budgeted Movies of the Year – *18*
1990 Academy Awards Selections – *18*
Top-Grossing Independently Produced Feature Films – *19*
Leading Independent Film Companies – *19*

 Television

Highest-Rated Network Television Series – *20*
1990 Emmy Award Selections – *20*
Highest-Rated Syndicated Series – *21*
Leading Cable Networks – *21*
Highest-Rated New Shows – *22*
Most Prolific Producers of Primetime Network Shows – *22*
Highest-Rated Television Shows of All Time – *22*
Highest-Rated Television Movies – *23*
Highest-Rated Television Specials – *23*
Highest-Rated Public Television Regularly Scheduled Series – *24*
Highest-Rated Public Television Specials or Limited Series – *24*

 Books

Longest-Running Hardcover Fiction Best-Sellers – *25*
Largest Publishers – *25*
Longest-Running Hardcover Nonfiction Best-Sellers – *26*
Longest-Running Trade Paperback Best-Sellers – *27*
Longest-Running Mass Market Paperback Best-Sellers – *27*

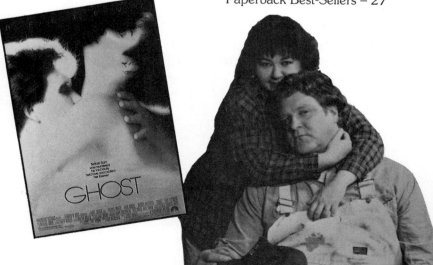

 Magazines

Magazines with the Highest Paid Circulation – *28*
Magazines with the Highest Advertising Revenue – *29*
Most Profitable Weeklies for Retailers – *30*
Most Profitable Monthlies for Retailers – *30*
Largest Magazine Publishing Companies – *31*

 Papers/Comics

Daily Newspapers with the Largest Circulation – *32*
Top Comic Book Series – *32*

 Radio

Top Radio Formats – *33*
Leading Radio Stations – *33*
Most Popular National Public Radio Programs – *33*

Theater

Top-Grossing Broadway Shows – *34*
1990 Tony Award Selections – *34*
Longest-Running Current Broadway Shows – *35*

 Home Video

Top Rental Videos – *36*
Best-Selling Home Videos – *37*
Best-Selling Non-Motion Picture Videos – *37*

 Sports

Most Popular Spectator Sports in America – *38*
Most Popular Participation Sports – *39*
Most-Watched Televised Sporting Events – *39*
Highest-Paid Athletes – *40*
Top Money Winners in Professional Sports:
  Tennis – *41*
  Golf – *41*
  Bowling – *41*
  Auto Racing – *41*
  Thoroughbred Racing – *41*
  Standardbred Racing – *41*
Top-Ranked College Basketball Teams – *42*
Top-Ranked College Football Teams – *42*
Baseball's Highest Batting Averages – *43*
Baseball's Highest Earned Run Averages – *43*
Football's Total Yards Rushing – *43*
Football's Quarterback Efficiency – *43*
Basketball's Highest Scoring Averages – *43*
Basketball's Highest Rebound Averages – *43*

 Leisure Time

Most-Preferred Leisure Time Pursuits – *44*
Most-Preferred Hobbies & Activities – *44*
Most Popular Forms of Gambling – *45*
Most Efficient Forms of Exercise – *45*

Business
Largest U.S. Industrial Corporations – 46
Largest U.S. Service Corporations – 46
Highest-Paid Show Business Personalities – 46
American Billionaires – 47
Largest Junk Bond Defaults – 47
Largest Black Enterprises – 48
Fastest-Growing Small Private Companies – 48
Most Valuable Corporations – 49
Highest-Paid Chief Executives – 49
Largest Industries – 50
Largest U.S. Exporters – 50
Top 10 Economic Indicators – 51
Biggest Business Deals – 52
The Big Board's Best-Performing Stocks – 52

 ## Advertising
Biggest-Spending National Advertisers – 53
National Ad Spending Ranked by Category – 53
Largest Advertising Agencies – 54
Top Mega-Brand Advertisers – 54
Leading Media Companies – 55
National Ad Spending Ranked by Media – 55

 ## Technology
Largest High-Technology Companies – 56
Best-Selling Home Electronics – 56
Best-Selling Personal Computers – 57
Best-Selling Personal Computer Software – 57

 ## Attractions
Most Popular Theme & Amusement Parks – 58
Most Popular Zoos – 59
Most Popular Aquariums – 59
Most Popular National Parks – 60
Biggest State & County Fairs – 61
Most Popular Water Parks – 61

 ## Shows
Highest-Grossing Variety/Specialty Acts – 62

 ## Kids' Entertainment
Best-Selling Children's Books – 63
Best-Selling Toys – 64
Largest Toy Companies – 64
Highest-Rated Television Series for Children 2-11 – 65
Best-Selling Kids' Home Videos – 65

 ## Consumer Products
Largest Department & Discount Store Retailers – 66
Leading Catalogs – 66
Best-Selling Cars in America – 67
Largest Consumer Product Companies – 68

Largest New Shopping Malls – 69
Top Specialty Retail Chains – 69
Largest Apparel Manufacturers – 70

 Eating & Drinking
Largest Fast-Food Chains – 71
Leading Types of Restaurants – 71
Best-Selling Grocery Store Items – 72
Restaurants Serving the Most People – 72
Most Popular Mixed Drinks – 73
Best-Selling Domestic Beers – 73

 Crime
The FBI's 10 Most Wanted Fugitives – 74
Cities with the Highest Violent Crime Rates – 75
Safest Metropolitan Areas in America – 75

 Travel
Largest Airlines – 76
Largest Hotel Chains – 76
Most Popular Domestic Destinations for Foreign Travelers in America – 77
Most Popular Foreign Destinations for American Travelers – 77

 College
Largest Universities – 78
Most Expensive Colleges – 78
Largest College Fraternities – 78

Most Popular Undergraduate Degrees – 79
Most Popular Master's Degrees – 79
Most Popular Doctoral Degrees – 80
Leading Foreign Student Enrollments – 80
Best-Selling Books on Campus Not on the Syllabus – 81

 Government
Largest Federal Departments & Agencies – 82
Top Recipients of U.S. Foreign Aid – 82
Best-Paid Jobs in the Federal Government – 83
Worst Attendance at Congressional Roll Call Votes – 83

 Demographics
Largest Cities – 84
Fastest-Growing Metro Areas – 80
Cities with Highest Earnings per Job – 85
Wealthiest Communities – 85

 Opinion
Biggest Box-Office Bombs – 86
Top 10 of The SPY 100 – 86
Blackwell's Worst-Dressed Women of the Year – 87
Most Livable Metropolitan Areas in America – 87
Top Environmental Priorities – 88
10 of the Most Endangered Species – 88
10 Milestones in the History of Popular Culture – 89

Notes to the Charts – 90
Any Suggestions? – 90
Index – 91

WHO SAYS?

The fundamental premise of *Top 10* is worth repeating: these charts are based on verifiable numbers...on the sales and attendance figures that spell success in American enterprise and popular culture. This is not a collection of some gonzo lists of 10 whatevers that we or someone else simply made up. We have gathered these numbers from the most credible sources we could find...from the acknowledged authorities who make it their business to know (the likes of *Billboard, Variety, Fortune*, Nielsen, *Publishers Weekly*, the FBI). In our "source" lines you'll see who says.

This is an annual almanac. It is an American chronicle based, in the huge majority of cases, on the events of 1990. We go to press in February so that we can report the year's actual (not projected) theater and movie box-office receipts, the season's final television ratings, concert attendance figures, circulation numbers, etc. Certain charts, notably those in the music, book and home video sections, are compiled from weekly surveys of stores and wholesalers; they are based on 1990 releases, and our compilations cover the full 52-week spectrum.

Bear in mind that corporate profits and sales figures reported in 1990 are based on the 1989 fiscal year (which also affects such compilations as the Fortune 500). However, our business charts based on stock valuations are calculated as of December 28, 1990, the last business day of the year.

Government data are, unfortunately, almost always a year old or more. And certain complex compilations (such as total retail sales or across-the-board sports attendance figures) are not available until several months after we go to press.

There are a few cases where chart data perforce include some estimated figures—and those are duly noted. And your understanding of certain other charts will benefit from the notes that appear on page 90.

All in all, this is the freshest statistical profile of American popular culture possible. We'll be back next year with a comprehensive update.

We hope you'll be back, too.

MUSIC

BEST-SELLING POP ALBUMS

Album/Label/Artist

1. **Janet Jackson's Rhythm Nation 1814** *(A&M)*
   Janet Jackson
2. **...But Seriously** *(Atlantic)*
   Phil Collins
3. **Soul Provider** *(Columbia)*
   Michael Bolton
4. **Pump** *(Geffen)*
   Aerosmith
5. **Please Hammer Don't Hurt 'Em** *(Capitol)*
   M.C. Hammer
6. **Forever Your Girl** *(Virgin)*
   Paula Abdul
7. **Dr. Feelgood** *(Elektra)*
   Motley Crue
8. **The End of the Innocence** *(Geffen)* Don Henley
9. **Cosmic Thing** *(Reprise)*
   The B-52's
10. **Storm Front** *(Columbia)*
    Billy Joel

*Source: BPI Communications, Inc. © 1991
Used with permission from Billboard
See note 1, page 90, for an explanation of Billboard charts*

Janet Jackson

READ THEIR LIPS

Ventriloquism is not a Grammy award category, Milli Vanilli learned when their "Best New Artist" Grammy was retrieved after the disclosure that Rob Pilatus and Fabrice Morvan were nowhere near the studio when "their" big hits, including "Girl You Know It's True," were cut. They can dance, but they can't sing. And no, the real singers on the album were not given the tainted Grammy.

MUSIC

Janet Jackson

BEST-SELLING RHYTHM & BLUES ALBUMS
Includes rap

Title/Label	Artist
1. Janet Jackson's Rhythm Nation 1814 *(A&M)*	Janet Jackson
2. Tender Lover *(Solar)*	Babyface
3. Please Hammer Don't Hurt 'Em *(Capitol)*	M.C. Hammer
4. After 7 *(Virgin)*	After 7
5. Stay with Me *(Columbia)*	Regina Belle
6. Back on the Block *(Qwest)*	Quincy Jones
7. Poison *(MCA)*	Bell Biv Devoe
8. Attitude *(Atlantic)*	Troop
9. Johnny Gill *(Motown)*	Johnny Gill
10. The Best of Luther Vandross: The Best of Love *(Epic)*	Luther Vandross

TOP RAP SINGLES

Title/Label	Artist
1. Expression *(Next Plateau)*	Salt-N-Pepa
2. The Humpty Dance *(Tommy Boy)*	Digital Underground
3. Buddy *(Tommy Boy)*	De La Soul
4. The Power *(Arista)*	Snap
5. Call Me D-Nice *(Jive)*	D-Nice
6. Beepers *(Nastymix)*	Sir Mix-A-Lot
7. Murder Rap *(Ruthless)*	Above the Law
8. Ownlee Eue *(Atlantic)*	Kwame & A New Beginning
9. Funhouse *(Select)*	Kid 'N Play
10. Me So Horny *(Skyywalker)*	2 Live Crew

Salt-N-Pepa

Source (both charts): BPI Communications, Inc.
© 1991. Used with permission from Billboard

RAP RAP

As Nasty as They Wanna Be, an album by the Miami rap group 2 Live Crew, was declared "obscene" by a federal judge in Florida. Then, a Ft. Lauderdale store owner was arrested for selling a copy of the album, and three members of the group were busted for performing their specialty sex raps.

The charges went to trial, and verdicts were emblematic of the eternal murkiness of obscenity trials: one conviction, one acquittal.

Record store bust.

BEST-SELLING JAZZ ALBUMS

Title/Label	Artist
1. Music from "When Harry Met Sally" (Columbia)	Harry Connick, Jr.
2. Waiting for Spring (GRP)	David Benoit
3. On Fire (Epic)	Michel Camilo
4. Standard Time Vol. 3 The Resolution of Romance (Columbia)	Wynton Marsalis
5. Remembrance (Verve)	The Harper Brothers
6. Deep in the Shed (Novus)	Marcus Roberts
7. Mood Indigo (Antilles)	Frank Morgan
8. We Are in Love (Columbia)	Harry Connick, Jr.
9. Reunion (GRP)	Gary Burton
10. Parallel Realities (MCA)	Jack DeJohnette

Harry Connick, Jr.

BEST-SELLING COUNTRY ALBUMS

Title/Label	Artist
1. Killin' Time (RCA)	Clint Black
2. No Holdin' Back (Warner Bros.)	Randy Travis
3. Pickin' on Nashville (Mercury)	The Kentucky Headhunters
4. Garth Brooks (Capitol)	Garth Brooks
5. Leave the Light On (RCA)	Lorrie Morgan
6. RVS III (Columbia)	Ricky Van Shelton
7. Simple Man (Epic)	The Charlie Daniels Band
8. Willow in the Wind (Mercury)	Kathy Mattea
9. The Boys Are Back (Capitol/Curb)	Sawyer Brown
10. Reba Live (MCA)	Reba McEntire

Source (both charts): BPI Communications, Inc.
© 1991. Used with permission from Billboard

Clint Black

NO TOOL, HE

M.C. Hammer, billowy jammers and all, leaped onto pop music's center stage this year and brought all of rap with him. With nearly 8 million copies sold, the most for any musician in 1990, the hyperkinetic Hammer (né Stanley Burrell of Oakland, CA) led rappers from the streets to the bank.

His biggest single of the year? "U Can't Touch This." Album *Please Hammer Don't Hurt 'Em* sold about 6 million copies. Altogether, M.C. Hammer nailed down the top spot on the charts for 21 weeks–the record for 1990.

MUSIC

BEST-SELLING MUSIC VIDEOS

Title/Label/Artist

1. **Hangin' Tough** *(CBS)*
   New Kids on the Block
2. **Hangin' Tough Live** *(CBS)*
3. **Janet Jackson's Rhythm Nation 1814** *(A&M)*
4. **Straight Up** *(Virgin)*
   Paula Abdul
5. **Milli Vanilli in Motion** *(6 West)*
6. **25X5: Continuing Adventures of the Rolling Stones** *(CBS)*
7. **Step by Step** *(CBS)*
   New Kids on the Block
8. **Kenny G Live** *(6 West)*
9. **Barry Manilow: Live on Broadway** *(6 West)*
10. **His Prerogative** *(MCA)*
    Bobby Brown

Source: BPI Communications, Inc. © 1991. Used with permission from Billboard

TOP-GROSSING CONCERT TOURS

Act	Total Gross	Total Attendance	No. of Shows	Sell-Outs
1. New Kids on the Block	$58,584,801	2,706,517	133	121
2. Paul McCartney	44,930,681	1,505,630	46	46
3. Billy Joel	41,670,036	1,752,664	91	89
4. Grateful Dead	27,923,513	1,304,864	60	50
5. Motley Crue	25,521,888	1,353,289	109	73
6. Janet Jackson	23,556,881	1,098,071	75	58
7. Aerosmith	23,383,600	1,111,109	83	42
8. Madonna	19,144,624	810,532	37	35
9. Phil Collins	19,144,510	778,603	45	38
10. Rolling Stones	18,837,313	661,921	12	12

Source: Amusement Business Magazine

Bette Midler

GRAMMY AWARDS: *1990 Selections*

Record: "Wind Beneath My Wings," Bette Midler
Album: *Nick of Time,* Bonnie Raitt
Pop Vocal Performance Duo or Group: "Don't Know Much," Linda Ronstadt & Aaron Neville
Pop Vocal Performance, Female: "Nick of Time," Bonnie Raitt
Pop Vocal Performance, Male: "How Am I Supposed to Live Without You?" Michael Bolton
Rock Vocal Performance Duo or Group: *Traveling Wilburys Volume One,* Traveling Wilburys
Rock Vocal Performance, Female: *Nick of Time,* Bonnie Raitt

TOP POP ARTISTS *Most charted singles and albums combined*

The Kids

1. New Kids on the Block
2. Janet Jackson
3. Phil Collins
4. Paula Abdul
5. Michael Bolton
6. M.C. Hammer
7. Aerosmith
8. Bell Biv Devoe
9. Taylor Dayne
10. Wilson Phillips

BEST-SELLING CLASSICAL ALBUMS

Title/Label	Artist
1. Horowitz at Home *(DG)*	Vladimir Horowitz
2. Horowitz: The Last Recording *(Sony Classical)*	Vladimir Horowitz
3. Horowitz in Moscow *(DG)*	Vladimir Horowitz
4. Beethoven: Symphony No. 9 *(DG)*	Leonard Bernstein
5. Tutto Pavarotti *(London)*	Luciano Pavarotti
6. Handel: Arias *(Angel)*	Kathleen Battle
7. Verdi & Puccini: Arias *(Sony Classical)*	Kiri Te Kanawa
8. The Movies Go to the Opera *(Angel)*	Various Artists
9. Black Angels *(Nonesuch)*	Kronos Quartet
10. Beethoven: 9 Symphonies *(RCA)*	Arturo Toscanini

Source (both charts): BPI Communications, Inc. © 1991. Used with permission from Billboard

Bonnie Raitt

Rhythm & Blues Vocal Performance, Male: "Every Little Step," Bobby Brown
Rhythm & Blues Vocal Performance, Female: *Giving You the Best That I Got*, Anita Baker
Rock Vocal Performance, Male: *The End of the Innocence*, Don Henley
Classical Album: *Bartok: Six String Quartets*, Emerson String Quartet
Jazz Instrumental Performance Duo or Group: *Chick Corea Akoustic Band*, Chick Corea Akoustic Band
Jazz Instrumental Performance, Soloist: *Aura*, Miles Davis

Source: Academy of Recording Arts and Sciences

MOVIES

TOP-GROSSING FEATURE FILMS
Domestic box office

Picture (Studio) Director	Stars	($ millions)
1. **Ghost** (*Paramount*) Jerry Zucker	Patrick Swayze, Demi Moore	$211.1
2. **Home Alone** (*20th Cent. Fox*) Chris Columbus	Macaulay Culkin	181.4
3. **Pretty Woman** (*Touchstone*) Gary Marshall	Julia Roberts, Richard Gere	178.3
4. **Teenage Mutant Ninja Turtles** (*New Line*) Steve Barron	Judith Hoage, Elias Koters	133.1
5. **The Hunt for Red October** (*Paramount*) John McTiernan	Sean Connery, Alec Baldwin	120.5
6. **Total Recall** (*Tri-Star*) Paul Verhoeven	Arnold Schwarzenegger	117.2
7. **Die Hard 2** (*20th Cent. Fox*) Renny Harlin	Bruce Willis, Bonnie Bedelia	115.3
8. **Dick Tracy** (*Touchstone*) Warren Beatty	Warren Beatty, Madonna	103.0
9. **Back to the Future III** (*Universal*) Robert Zemeckis	Michael J. Fox, Christopher Lloyd	86.5
10. **Presumed Innocent** (*Warner Bros.*) Alan Pakula	Harrison Ford, Bonnie Bedelia	86.0

Source: Baseline II Inc.

TOP-GROSSING FILMS OF ALL TIME
It's now a 200-million-dollar club

1.	**E.T.**	$367.7 million
2.	**Star Wars**	322.7 million
3.	**Return of the Jedi**	263.7 million
4.	**Batman**	251.2 million
5.	**Jaws**	245.0 million
6.	**Raiders of the Lost Ark**	242.4 million
7.	**Beverly Hills Cop**	234.8 million
8.	**Empire Strikes Back**	223.2 million
9.	**Ghostbusters**	221.1 million
10.	**Ghost**	211.1 million

Source: Baseline II Inc.

MOVIE STUDIOS RANKED BY MARKET SHARE

Percentage of domestic box office

Distributor	Share
1. Buena Vista (Disney)	15.5%
2. Paramount	14.9
3. Universal	13.1
3. 20th Century Fox	13.1
3. Warner Bros.	13.1
6. Tri-Star	9.0
7. Orion	5.6
8. Columbia Pictures	4.9
9. New Line Cinema	4.4
10. MGM/UA	2.8

Source: Baseline II Inc.

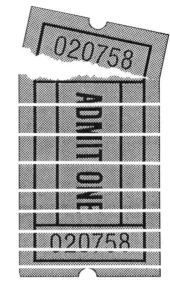

Arnold

Meryl

HIGHEST-PAID ACTORS AND ACTRESSES

Star	$ millions
1. Arnold Schwarzenegger	$30
2. Bruce Willis	28
2. Sean Connery	28
4. Eddie Murphy	25
5. Sylvester Stallone	24
6. Michael J. Fox	22
7. Tom Cruise	18
8. Harrison Ford	13
9. Meryl Streep	9
9. Mel Gibson	9

Source: An average of the highest reported figures we could find, blended with a healthy dose of industry insider gossip as to the deals going down this year in Hollywood.

MGM/UA/IOU

Another hunk of Hollywood floated offshore in 1990 as Italian Giancarlo Parretti bought MGM/UA from Kirk Kerkorian for a reported price of $1.3 billion and merged it with his Pathé Communications. With most rights to the film libraries of MGM/UA, Cannon and Pathé already sold, the highly leveraged deal enriched a few executives but left the combined companies strapped for cash and sources of income.

MOVIES

TOP-GROSSING FOREIGN FILMS IN AMERICA

Cinema Paradiso

	Picture	Country	Gross ($ millions)
1.	Cinema Paradiso	Italy	$11.4
2.	The Cook, The Thief, His Wife and Her Lover	England	7.4
3.	Tie Me Up, Tie Me Down	Spain	3.9
4.	Camille Claudel	France	3.3
5.	The Krays	England	2.0
6.	Dreams	Japan	1.9
7.	Too Beautiful for You	France	1.8
8.	Jesus of Montreal	Canada	1.6
8.	May Fools	France	1.6
10.	Monsieur Hiré	France	1.4

HIGHEST-BUDGETED* MOVIES OF THE YEAR

	Picture/Studio	Budget ($ millions)
1.	**Die Hard 2** (20th Century Fox)	$60
2.	**Total Recall** (Tri-Star)	50
2.	**Godfather III** (Paramount)	50
4.	**Havana** (Universal)	45
4.	**Days of Thunder** (Paramount)	45
4.	**Another 48 Hours** (Paramount)	45
7.	**Back to the Future III** (Universal)	40
8.	**Dick Tracy** (Touchstone)	35
8.	**Gremlins II** (Warner Bros.)	35
10.	**The Hunt for Red October** (Paramount)	30

*These are estimated negative costs, and do not include prints, advertising or other distribution expenses.

Source (both charts): Baseline II Inc.

Dan Aykroyd, Jessica Tandy and Morgan Freeman, stars of **Driving Miss Daisy**.

ACADEMY AWARDS:
1990 Selections

Best Picture: *Driving Miss Daisy*

Best Director: Oliver Stone, *Born on the Fourth of July*

Best Actor: Daniel Day Lewis, *My Left Foot*

Best Actress: Jessica Tandy, *Driving Miss Daisy*

Best Supporting Actor: Denzel Washington, *Glory*

Best Supporting Actress: Brenda Fricker, *My Left Foot*

Turtle star Raphel ponders an escape plan.

TOP-GROSSING INDEPENDENTLY PRODUCED FEATURE FILMS

Picture	Distributor	Gross ($ millions)
1. Teenage Mutant Ninja Turtles	New Line	$133.1
2. House Party	New Line	26.1
3. Wild at Heart	Goldwyn	14.5
4. Pump Up the Volume	New Line	11.5
5. Cinema Paradiso	Miramax	11.4
6. The Cook, The Thief, His Wife and Her Lover	Miramax	7.4
7. Leatherface: Texas Chainsaw Massacre III	New Line	5.8
8. A Shock to the System	Corsair	4.1
8. Heart Condition	New Line	4.1
10. Camille Claudel	Orion Classics	4.0

Source: Baseline II Inc.

LEADING INDEPENDENT FILM COMPANIES

Ranked by 1990 estimated total box-office gross (in millions)

1. New Line Cinema $170.0
2. Miramax Films 27.0
3. Samuel Goldwyn Co. 20.0
4. Cinecom Entertainment 7.0
5. Concorde Pictures 5.3
6. Corsair Films $5.0
7. Hemdale Film Corp. 4.5
8. Avenue Pictures 3.3
9. Taurus Entertainment 3.0
10. Skouras Pictures 1.8

Source: Baseline II Inc.

Best Screenplay (Original): Tom Schulman, *Dead Poets Society*
Best Cinematography: Freddie Francis, *Glory*
Best Art Direction: Anton Furst and Peter Young, *Batman*
Best Film Editing: David Brenner, Joe Hutshing, *Born on the Fourth of July*
Best Original Music Score: Alan Menken, *The Little Mermaid*
Best Original Song: Alan Menken and Howard Ashman, "Under the Sea" in *The Little Mermaid*
Best Visual Effects: John Bruno, Dennis Muren, Hoyt Yeatman, Dennis Skotak, *The Abyss*
Best Foreign Film: *Cinema Paradiso* (Italy)

Source: National Academy of Recording Arts and Sciences

TELEVISION

HIGHEST-RATED NETWORK TELEVISION SERIES

The year's top two shows are both produced by the same outfit—the Carsey Werner Co.

Program	Network	Rating	Share
1. Roseanne	ABC	23.4	25
2. Bill Cosby Show	NBC	23.1	38
3. Cheers	NBC	22.9	36
4. A Different World	NBC	21.1	34
5. America's Funniest Home Videos	ABC	21.0	32
6. Golden Girls	NBC	20.1	35
7. 60 Minutes	CBS	19.7	33
8. Wonder Years	ABC	19.2	29
9. Empty Nest	NBC	19.1	33
10. Chicken Soup	ABC	18.2	29

"Rating" represents the percentage of **all** households tuned to the show. "Share" represents the percentage of households with television **sets in use** tuned to the show. Source: Nielsen Media Research. See note 2, page 90 for more information on Nielsen ratings

Above: The Cosby Show cast/Roseanne Barr and John Goodman of Roseanne.

Candice Bergen

EMMY AWARDS:
1990 Selections

Comedy Series: Murphy Brown (CBS)
Drama Series: L.A. Law (NBC)
Mini Series: Drug Wars: The Camarena Story (NBC)
Drama/Comedy Special: "Caroline?" Hallmark Hall of Fame (CBS)
Lead Actor, Comedy Series: Ted Danson, Cheers (NBC)
Lead Actress, Comedy Series: Candice Bergen, Murphy Brown (CBS)
Lead Actress, Drama: Patricia Wettig, thirty something (ABC)

Vanna White and Pat Sajak.

HIGHEST-RATED SYNDICATED SERIES

Program	Supplier	Rating
1. Wheel of Fortune	King World/Camelot	14.5
2. Jeopardy!	King World/Camelot	12.7
3. Star Trek	Paramount Pictures	10.0
4. Bill Cosby Show	Viacom	9.5
5. Oprah Winfrey Show	King World/Camelot	9.4
6. Current Affair	20th Cent. Fox/LBS	8.8
6. Wheel of Fortune (Wknd.)	King World/Camelot	8.8
8. Universal Pictures Debut Network	MCA-TV	8.7
9. Entertainment Tonight	Teletrib	8.4
10. Columbia Night at the Movies	Teletrib	7.0

Source: Nielsen Media Research

PHOTO: RON SLENZAK PHOTOGRAPHY INC. COURTESY OF MERV GRIFFIN ENTERPRISES

LEADING CABLE NETWORKS

Network	Subscribers (in millions)
1. ESPN	55.9
2. CNN	54.4
3. TBS SuperStation	54.0
4. USA Network	51.5
5. Nickelodeon/Nick at Nite	50.8
6. MTV	50.4
7. The Nashville Network	50.0
8. C-SPAN	49.7
8. The Discovery Channel	49.7
10. The Family Channel	49.1

Source: National Cable TV Association, National Cable Network Directory

Lead Actor, Drama: Peter Falk, *Columbo* (ABC)

Lead Actor, Mini Series or Special: Hume Cronyn, *Age-Old Friends* (HBO)

Lead Actress, Mini Series or Special: Barbara Hershey, *A Killing in a Small Town* (CBS)

Writing/Comedy Series: Bob Brush, "Goodbye," *The Wonder Years* (ABC)

Writing/Drama Series: David Keiley, "Blood, Sweat, and Fears," *L.A. Law* (NBC)

Writing/Mini Series or Special: Terrence McNally, "Andre's Mother" *American Playhouse* (PBS)

Directing, Comedy Series: Michael Dinner, "Goodbye," *The Wonder Years* (ABC)

Directing, Drama Series: Thorance Carter, *Equal Justice: Promises to Keep* (ABC)

Directing, Mini Series or Special: Joseph Sargent, "Caroline?" *Hallmark Hall of Fame* (CBS)

Source: Academy of Television Arts and Sciences

TELEVISION

HIGHEST-RATED NEW SHOWS
Year-end ranking

Show	Network	Rating	Share	Rank
1. America's Funniest People	ABC	16.6	25	11
2. Fresh Prince of Bel Air	NBC	13.1	21	36
3. Law and Order	NBC	12.7	23	40
4. Married People	ABC	12.7	21	41
5. Trials of Rosie O'Neill	CBS	11.4	20	48
6. Evening Shade	CBS	11.2	20	50
7. Ferris Bueller	NBC	11.2	17	51
8. Going Places	ABC	11.0	20	54
9. Uncle Buck	CBS	11.0	18	55
10. American Dreamer	NBC	10.3	20	63

Source: Nielsen Television Index Ranking Report. See note 2, page 90

David Coulier and Arleen Sorkin, hosts of America's Funniest People.

MOST PROLIFIC PRODUCERS OF PRIMETIME NETWORK SHOWS

Producer	Prime Time Hours per Week
1. Lorimar Productions	11.0
2. Columbia Pictures TV	5.5
2. Paramount Network TV	5.5
2. Warner Bros.	5.5
5. Steven J. Cannell Productions	5.0
5. Universal Television	5.0
7. 20th Century Fox	4.0
8. MGM/UA TV	3.5
9. NBC Productions	3.0
9. Viacom Productions	3.0

Larry Hagman, star of Lorimar Productions' Dallas.

HIGHEST-RATED TELEVISION SHOWS OF ALL TIME

1. **M*A*S*H,** final episode, 2/28/83
2. **Dallas,** "Who Shot JR?" 11/21/80
3. **Roots,** episode 8, 1/30/77
4. **Super Bowl XVI,** 1982
5. **Super Bowl XVII,** 1983
6. **Super Bowl XX,** 1986
7. **Gone With the Wind,** Part I, 11/7/76
8. **Gone With the Wind,** Part II, 11/8/76
9. **Super Bowl XII,** 1978
10. **Super Bowl XIII,** 1979

It's a wrap on the set of M*A*S*H.

HIGHEST-RATED TELEVISION MOVIES

Title	Network	Rating	Share
1. Small Sacrifices, Part 2	ABC	25.2	39
2. Blind Faith, Part 2	NBC	23.3	36
3. Twin Peaks	ABC	21.7	33
4. A Cry for Help: Tracy Thurman Story	NBC	21.5	33
5. AT&T Presents: The Incident	CBS	20.8	33
6. Blind Faith, Part 1	NBC	19.9	31
7. The Operation	CBS	19.8	30
8. Gunsmoke: Last Apache	CBS	19.7	32
9. Hallmark: Caroline?	CBS	19.4	30
10. False Witness	NBC	18.7	29

Source: Nielsen Media Research

HIGHEST-RATED TELEVISION SPECIALS

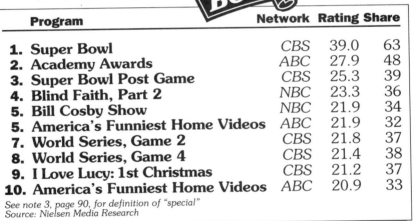

Program	Network	Rating	Share
1. Super Bowl	CBS	39.0	63
2. Academy Awards	ABC	27.9	48
3. Super Bowl Post Game	CBS	25.3	39
4. Blind Faith, Part 2	NBC	23.3	36
5. Bill Cosby Show	NBC	21.9	34
5. America's Funniest Home Videos	ABC	21.9	32
7. World Series, Game 2	CBS	21.8	37
8. World Series, Game 4	CBS	21.4	38
9. I Love Lucy: 1st Christmas	CBS	21.2	37
10. America's Funniest Home Videos	ABC	20.9	33

See note 3, page 90, for definition of "special"
Source: Nielsen Media Research

GH SCRUBS UP

General Hospital (ABC), now in its 27th year, is still busy chronicling the loves, marriages (seven in 1990, along with four engagements, one birth and eight deaths), affairs, tensions, ambitions and betrayals that characterize–and wonderfully complicate–life in Port Charles. This was the year the sets got redecorated, a new character (Casey) materialized from outer space, and another character (Duke) managed to die twice.

First aired in April 1963, *GH* has occupied the top spot among daytime dramas since 1979.

ILLUSTRATION: ALAN WEISS

TELEVISION

HIGHEST-RATED PUBLIC TELEVISION SERIES
Regularly scheduled

Program	Rating	No. of Stations	Coverage
1. National Geographic Specials	4.9	300	97%
2. This Old House	4.6	306	96
3. Nature	3.9	288	93
4. Frugal Gourmet	3.8	291	95
5. Nova	3.5	285	94
6. Mystery!	3.4	291	95
7. Mark Russell Specials	2.9	298	97
8. Wild America	2.8	274	87
9. Sesame Street	2.7	309	98
10. Adventure	2.6	247	89

The Civil War, produced by filmmaker Ken Burns, was far and away the highest-rated limited series ever broadcast on PBS.

HIGHEST-RATED PUBLIC TELEVISION PROGRAMS
Specials or limited series

Program	Rating	No. of Stations	Coverage
1. The Civil War	8.8	309	98%
2. Miracle Planet	3.7	301	96
3. Stalin	2.6	287	91
4. Eyes on the Prize II	2.3	286	95
5. Moyers: The Public Mind	2.2	269	91
6. Inside Gorbachev's USSR	2.1	258	93
7. Skyscraper	1.9	233	86
8. Art of the Western World	1.9	293	96
9. World Without Walls	1.3	239	90
10. Routes of Rhythm	1.2	199	75

Source (both charts): Nielsen Television Index and PBS Research

PEAKS...AND VALLEYS

Drawn by director David Lynch's signature non-sequitur visual style, and by the question of which among his mumbling, thousand-yard-stare characters had actually offed Laura Palmer, viewers made ABC's quirky prime-time soap *Twin Peaks* the hottest show at midyear. Laura's dad did the deed, we learned in the fall, but by then *TP* had settled down to around 75th in the ratings. What happened? Well, ABC shifted the show to traditional-graveyard Saturday night; and maybe Lynch's novel peculiarities just evolved into familiar peculiarities.

BOOKS

Longest-Running Hardcover
FICTION BEST-SELLERS

Title	Author	Publisher	Weeks on List
1. Oh, The Places You'll Go!	Dr. Seuss	Random House	37
2. Clear and Present Danger	Tom Clancy	Putnam	28
3. The Stand: The Complete and Uncut Edition	Stephen King	Doubleday	27
3. The Burden of Proof	Scott Turow	Farrar, Straus & Giroux	27
5. The Bourne Ultimatum	Robert Ludlum	Random House	24
6. September	Rosamunde Pilcher	St. Martin's/ Dunne	22
7. Message from Nam	Danielle Steel	Delacorte	18
7. Memories of Midnight	Sidney Sheldon	Morrow	17
9. An Inconvenient Woman	Dominick Dunne	Crown	17
10. Devices and Desires	P.D. James	Knopf	16

Source: Reprinted from the (above) January 4, 1991 and (below) December 21, 1990 issues of Publishers Weekly, published by Cahners Publishing Company, a division of Reed Publishing U.S.A. © 1990 by Reed Publishing U.S.A.

LARGEST PUBLISHERS

Company	Revenues ($ millions)
1. Simon & Schuster	$1,320 (est.)
2. Time Publishing Group	1,140
3. Harcourt Brace Jovanovich	885
4. Random House	850
5. Reader's Digest	844
6. McGraw-Hill	740
7. Encyclopaedia Britannica	650
8. Bantam Doubleday Dell	630
9. Times Mirror Corp.	575
10. The Thomson Corp.	598

MS. DEAL

Ivana Trump once again demonstrates that when it comes to cutting a deal with an American book publisher, there are just three things you need: fame, fame, and fame. Forget about talent, writing ability, and something to say. Trump's agent, William Morris, got her a two-book deal—both to be "commercial" novels—with Pocket Books (for a widely rumored cool $1 million). Yes, a co-writer will work with Ms. Trump.

Source: N.Y. Times, Oct. 6, 1990

BOOKS

Longest-Running Hardcover
NONFICTION BEST-SELLERS

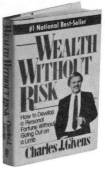

Title	Author	Publisher	Weeks on List
1. Wealth Without Risk	Charles Givens	Simon & Schuster	41
2. Barbarians at the Gate: The Fall of RJR Nabisco	Bryan Burrough & John Helyar	HarperCollins	36
3. Megatrends 2000	John Naisbitt & Patrician Aburdene	Morrow	33
4. It Was on Fire When I Lay Down on It	Robert Fulghum	Villard Books	31
5. Liar's Poker: Rising Through the Wreckage on Wall Street	Michael M. Lewis	Norton	30
6. Men at Work	George F. Will	Macmillan	26
7. Dave Barry Turns 40	Dave Barry	Crown	21
7. You Just Don't Understand: Men and Women in Conversation	Deborah Tannen	Morrow	21
9. Homecoming: Reclaiming and Championing Your Inner Child	John Bradshaw	Bantam	20
9. All I Really Need to Know I Learned in Kindergarten	Robert Fulghum	Villard Books	20

Source: Reprinted from the January 4, 1991 issue of Publishers Weekly, published by Cahners Publishing Company, a division of Reed Publishing U.S.A. © 1990 by Reed Publishing U.S.A.

EVANS IN, EVANS OUT

In 1990, scorecard changes in the S.I. Newhouse publishing arena (Condé Nast magazines, Random House books, etc.) were as follows: Joni Evans, erstwhile and very successful publisher at Random House, got dealt away to run her own little imprint within RH. Her successor is Harry Evans, the whimsical and wildly unpredictable charter editor of *Condé Nast Traveler* (and not incidentally the spouse of Tina Brown, who as editor has made a major success of *Vanity Fair,* another Condé Nast publication).

What kind of game will Harry play at Random House books? Well, his background is Brit newspapers (*The Sunday Times* and *The Times of London*), where he had monumental clashes with owner Rupert Murdoch. Now, as chief at Random House, Harry inherits a deal to publish the memoirs of the selfsame Murdoch.

Harry Evans

Longest-Running TRADE PAPERBACK BEST-SELLERS

Title	Author	Publisher	Weeks on List
1. Codependent No More	Melody Beattie	H&R/Hazelden	51
2. The T-Factor Fat Gram Counter	Jamie Pope Cordle/ Martin Katahn	Norton	45
3. 50 Simple Things You Can Do to Save the Earth	EarthWorks Group	EarthWorks Press	31
4. Weirdos from Another Planet	Bill Watterson	Andrews & McMeel	29
5. Dianetics (Rev. Ed.)	L. Ron Hubbard	Bridge	21
6. From Beirut to Jerusalem	Thomas Friedman	Doubleday/ Anchor	16
7. Happy Trails!	Berke Breathed	Little, Brown	15
7. A Brief History of Time	Stephen W. Hawking	Bantam	15
9. The Road Less Traveled	M. Scott Peck	Touchstone/S&S	14
10. The Authoritative Calvin & Hobbes	Bill Watterson	Andrews & McMeel	12

Longest-Running MASS-MARKET PAPERBACK BEST-SELLERS

Title	Author	Publisher	Weeks on List
1. All I Really Need to Know I Learned in Kindergarten	Robert Fulghum	Villard Books	50
2. The Joy Luck Club	Amy Tan	Ivy Books	25
3. Presumed Innocent	Scott Turow	Warner	21
4. Clear and Present Danger	Tom Clancy	Berkley	15
5. The Pillars of the Earth	Ken Follett	Nal/Signet	13
5. The Hunt for Red October	Tom Clancy	Berkley	13
7. The Dark Half	Stephen King	Nal/Signet	12
7. The Oldest Living Confederate Widow Tells All	Allen Gurganus	Ivy Books	12
7. While My Pretty One Sleeps	Mary Higgins Clark	Pocket Books	12
7. The Russia House	John le Carré	Bantam	12

Source (both charts): Reprinted from the January 4, 1991 issue of Publishers Weekly, published by Cahners Publishing Company, a division of Reed Publishing U.S.A. © 1990 by Reed Publishing U.S.A.

ADVANCE MEN

Not so long ago, only a handful of authors could command a million-dollar advance. By 1990, fully 50 authors were writing under the bright lights of a seven-figure deal. The fattest advances of the year went to Ken Follett ($12.3 million from Dell for two books) and to Jeffrey Archer (over $20 million from HarperCollins for three books). Such proven best-selling authors—including Tom Clancy, with over 40 million books in print—now get advances that exceed the selling prices of some publishing houses. Industry observers blame the money paid to writers for the perennial woes of the publishing business; few point to the debts of leveraged buyouts or to the sluggish productivity of many publishers.

Sources: N.Y. Times, Wall Street Journal, Publishers Weekly

Ken Follett

MAGAZINES

MAGAZINES WITH THE HIGHEST PAID CIRCULATION

Combined newsstand and subscription

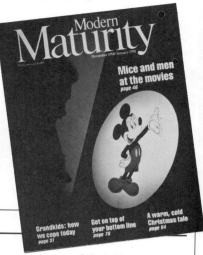

Title/Circulation	
1. Modern Maturity	22,443,464
2. Reader's Digest	16,396,919
3. TV Guide	15,837,064
4. National Geographic	10,182,911
5. Better Homes & Gardens	8,002,895
6. Family Circle	5,159,147
7. Good Housekeeping	5,105,094
8. Ladies' Home Journal	5,022,414
9. McCall's	5,011,473
10. Woman's Day	4,612,833

Source: Magazine Publishers of America

UPSTARTS, RERUNS AND SHUTDOWNS

Some 535 new American consumer magazines started up in 1990 and about 60% of them failed during 1990. Three cases (two failures): *Men's Life, Egg,* and *Entertainment Weekly. Men's Life,* launched by Murdoch Magazines, debuted with an issue containing just about every old idea and department that anyone could remember running in a publication for men, except one: pretty girls. ML editor Barry Golson called it "essentially *Playboy* without the nudes."

Egg demonstrated a hard-

MAGAZINES WITH THE HIGHEST ADVERTISING REVENUE

Monthlies barely stand a chance

Title/Revenue	
1. Time	$373,385,017
2. Sports Illustrated	336,671,529
3. People Weekly	325,201,199
4. TV Guide	322,985,623
5. Business Week	260,575,042
6. Newsweek	255,918,694
7. Fortune	187,284,536
8. Forbes	157,696,940
9. U.S. News & World Report	152,843,252
10. Better Homes & Gardens	152,438,109

Source: Publishers Information Bureau

boiled fact of publishing life: you can't be too rich. Bankrolled by the Forbes organization, it wasn't easy to say what *Egg* was. Best I.D.? Uptown staff trying to do a downtown mag. Less than a week into 1991, *Egg* cracked.

Entertainment Weekly demonstrates another truism: it helps to have a new idea once in a while. But launchers at Time, Inc., keep trying to repeat their success with *People* by republishing the same mag under a new name. At year's end, *EW* is still breathing.

MAGAZINES

MOST PROFITABLE MAGAZINES FOR RETAILERS
Success at the newsstand

TOP WEEKLIES

Title	Monthly Retailer Profits
1. TV Guide	$4,534,174
2. People Weekly	2,747,131
3. National Enquirer	2,667,571
4. The Star	2,148,086
5. Woman's World	1,336,904
6. Globe	862,848
7. National Examiner	598,308
8. Weekly World News	490,683
9. Time	426,829
10. Sports Illustrated	401,027

TOP MONTHLIES

Title	Monthly Retailer Profits
1. Penthouse	$1,225,168
2. Cosmopolitan	1,085,499
3. First for Woman	691,167
4. Playboy	666,061
5. Glamour	649,631
6. Good Housekeeping	540,185
7. Vogue	449,959
8. Muscle & Fitness	393,155
9. Ladies' Home Journal	354,657
10. Reader's Digest	343,224

Source (both charts): Magazine & Bookseller, based on data reported by the Audit Bureau of Circulations and Business Publications Audit

SKIN TRADE

The weirdest trade magazine start-up was probably *U.S. Stripper*, a bimonthly serving the exotic dance "industry" with articles on dancing, sound equipment, top stars like Amber Lynn, and guides to clubs and booking agents. It wobbled over the border from Canada carrying photographic advertisements from improbably swollen dancers with names like Beverly Hills and Melisa Mounds. Our favorite? Heidi Hooters. *U.S. Stripper* is well over the line into grotesquerie.

Below: 10 of the top titles published by Time Warner.

LARGEST MAGAZINE PUBLISHING COMPANIES

Ranked by revenue

Company	Magazine Revenue ($ millions)
1. Time Warner	$1,855.0
2. Hearst Corp.	992.5
3. Advance Publications	841.9
4. Thomson Corp.	733.1
5. News Corp.	713.0
6. Reader's Digest	589.4
7. Reed Publishing USA	580.0
8. McGraw-Hill	460.0
9. International Data Group	420.0
10. Meredith Corp.	417.1

Source: © 1991 Crain Communications Inc.
Reprinted from the June 25, 1990 issue of *Advertising Age*

CALL IT "FULL-FIGURED"

Heaviest magazine of the year (we're talking poundage, not content): *Bride's*, weighing in with a 3¾-pound February/March issue of 1,034 pages, at least 875 of them ads for one-time dresses, dishes, glasses and beaches. (Maybe more—it's often difficult to distinguish edit and advertising.)

Never mind that America has the highest divorce rate in the developed world. Hope–and advertising–evidently spring eternal.

PAPERS/COMICS

LARGEST DAILY NEWSPAPERS

Newspaper	Average Daily Circulation
1. Wall Street Journal (nat'l ed.)	1,857,131
2. USA Today	1,347,450
3. Los Angeles Times	1,196,323
4. New York Times	1,108,477
5. New York Daily News*	1,097,693
6. Washington Post	780,532
7. Chicago Tribune	721,067
8. Newsday (all day)	714,128
9. Detroit Free Press	636,182
10. San Francisco Chronicle	562,887

*Pre-strike data; see item below
Source: Editor & Publisher

TOP COMIC BOOK SERIES

Title/Publisher

1. Spider-Man *(Marvel)*
2. Legend of the Dark Knight *(DC)*
3. Batman *(DC)*
4. Robin *(DC)*
5. Aliens v. Predators *(Dark Horse)*
6. X-Men *(Marvel)*
7. Fantastic Four *(Marvel)*
8. Amazing Spider-Man *(Marvel)*
9. Punisher War Journal *(Marvel)*
10. Wolverine *(Marvel)*

Source: Capital City Distribution, Inc.

Published in 1990, the premier issue of the new Spider-Man series, written and drawn by Todd McFarlane, sold 2,786,000 copies – the best-selling comic book in U.S. history.

DAILY NEWS STRIKE

For high and low drama, the strike at the New York *Daily News*, America's third largest metropolitan daily newspaper, is tough to match outside Hollywood. It has featured truck-burning, scab-stabbing, riots, and speechifying by governors and bishops, plus charges and countercharges of "union-busting" and "Who's running this paper, anyway?"

RADIO

TOP RADIO FORMATS

Format	No. of Stations
1. Country	2,452
2. Adult Contemporary	2,135
3. Top 40	824
4. Religion	745
5. Oldies	659
6. Rock (Album, Modern, Classic)	429
7. News/Talk	405
8. Adult Standards	383
9. Spanish and Ethnic	342
10. Urban, Black	294

Source: M Street Radio Directory

MOST POPULAR NATIONAL PUBLIC RADIO PROGRAMS

Program	Audience*
1. Morning Edition	4,993,800
2. All Things Considered (weekday)	4,911,700
3. Weekend Edition (Sat.)	1,399,800
4. Fresh Air	1,155,000
5. Weekend Edition (Sun.)	923,000
6. Car Talk	857,900
7. All Things Considered (Sat.)	629,100
8. All Things Considered (Sun.)	509,900
9. Performance Today	287,500
10. McPartland's Piano Jazz	264,200

*Weekly cume persons
Source: National Public Radio

LEADING RADIO STATIONS

1. **WINS-AM** New York
2. **WHTZ-FM** New York
3. **WCBS-AM** New York
4. **KIIS-AM/FM** Los Angeles
5. **WPLJ-FM** New York
6. **WCBS-FM** New York
7. **KOST-FM** Los Angeles
8. **WXRK-FM** New York
9. **WLTW-FM** New York
10. **WPAT-AM/FM** New York

Source: © 1990, The Arbitron Company

LISTEN UP!

Ol' Claude is the real guy among a host of radio personalities including Old Man Schultz, Lester Longmire, Claude the Cat, of course, and Little Alf. Claude Tomlinson, that is, the host of *Morning Drive* on WIVK-AM in Knoxville, TN—arguably the most successful local deejay in the country. He captivates 41.7% of the Knoxville radio audience, and he's had a lot of practice: Ol' Claude signed the station on the air hisself back in 19 and 53.

THEATER

TOP-GROSSING BROADWAY SHOWS

Show	Box Office
1. Phantom of the Opera	$30,262,651
2. Les Misérables	26,225,340
3. City of Angels	24,737,501
4. Cats	22,941,820
5. Gypsy	21,941,875
6. Grand Hotel	19,048,828
7. Jerome Robbins' Broadway	15,778,978
8. Black and Blue	15,229,110
9. Aspects of Love	13,823,414
10. Lettice and Lovage	11,373,451

Source: Compiled by Top 10 from weekly box-office reports as published in Variety

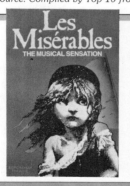

TONY AWARD WINNERS: *1990 Selections*

Play: The Grapes of Wrath
Musical: City of Angels
Revival: Gypsy
Lead Actor (Play): Robert Morse, Tru
Lead Actress (Play): Maggie Smith, Lettice and Lovage
Lead Actor (Musical): James Naughton, City of Angels
Lead Actress (Musical): Tyne Daly, Gypsy
Director (Play): Frank Galati, The Grapes of Wrath
Director (Musical): Tommy Tune, Grand Hotel
Scenic Design: Robin Wagner, City of Angels
Costume Design: Santo Loquasto, Grand Hotel
Lighting Design: Jules Fisher, Grand Hotel
Choreography: Tommy Tune, Grand Hotel

Source: The Antoinette Perry Awards

LONGEST-RUNNING CURRENT BROADWAY SHOWS

Number of performances as of December 30, 1990

1.	Cats	3,437
2.	Les Misérables	1,527
3.	Phantom of the Opera	1,224
4.	Black and Blue	805
5.	Grand Hotel	473
6.	Gypsy	468
7.	A Few Good Men	465
8.	City of Angels	439
9.	Aspects of Love	305
10.	Piano Lesson	295

Source: Variety

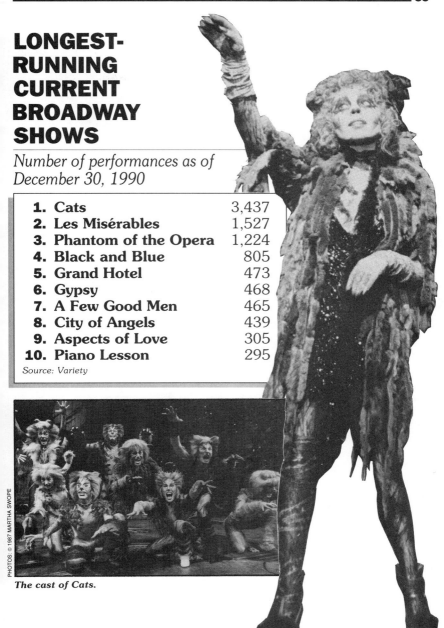

The cast of Cats.

THE END OF THE LINE

A Chorus Line, Broadway's all-time longest running show (and second most profitable), finally went dark at the end of March after some 6,100 performances. It opened on July 25, 1975, at the Shubert Theatre, and along the way won the Pulitzer, the Drama Critics Circle Award and numerous Tonys.

It will be on the road forever.

HOME VIDEO

TOP RENTAL VIDEOS

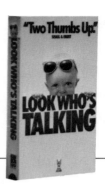

Picture Director	Stars
1. **Look Who's Talking** Amy Heckerling	John Travolta, Kirstie Alley
2. **When Harry Met Sally** Rob Reiner	Billy Crystal, Meg Ryan
3. **Parenthood** Ron Howard	Steve Martin, Rick Moranis, Martha Plimpton, Mary Steenburgen
4. **K-9** Rod Daniel	James Belushi, Jerry Lee, Mel Harris
5. **Dead Poets Society** Peter Weir	Robin Williams
6. **Steel Magnolias** Herbert Ross	Olympia Dukakis, Sally Field, Daryl Hannah, Dolly Parton, Shirley MacLaine, Julia Roberts
7. **Sea of Love** Harold Becker	Al Pacino, Ellen Barkin, John Goodman
8. **Turner & Hooch** Roger Spottiswoode	Tom Hanks, Hooch
9. **Black Rain** Ridley Scott	Michael Douglas, Andy Garcia, Ken Takakura, Kate Capshaw
10. **Internal Affairs** Mike Figgis	Richard Gere, Andy Garcia

Source: BPI Communications, Inc. ©1991. Used with permission from Billboard

Big kids on the block.

VIDEO BOOM

With the VCR fast approaching "necessity" status (nearly three-quarters of U.S. households own at least one), videotape rental/sales has become a megabusiness. In fact, it brings in nearly twice as much money as movie theaters.

Top operator in a fast-consolidating field is Blockbuster Entertainment Corp. of Ft. Lauderdale, FL, with some 1,500 stores. Its advantage over some 30,000 mom-and-pop video shops is a lesson in capitalism: Blockbuster's "Superstores" offer a bigger selection (10,000 titles), longer hours (7 days, till midnight) and lower prices.

BEST-SELLING HOME VIDEOS

1. **Bambi**
   Walt Disney Home Video
2. **New Kids on the Block: Hangin' Tough Live**
   CBS Music Video Enterprises
3. **The Little Mermaid**
   Walt Disney Home Video
4. **Lethal Weapon 2**
   Warner Home Video
5. **The Wizard of Oz: 50th Anniv. Ed.**
   MGM/UA Home Video
6. **Batman**
   Warner Home Video
7. **Honey, I Shrunk the Kids**
   Walt Disney Home Video
8. **The Land Before Time**
   MCA/Universal Home Video
9. **Who Framed Roger Rabbit**
   Touchstone Home Video
10. **Teenage Mutant Ninja Turtles: Cowabunga, Shredhead**
    Family Home Entertainment

Source: BPI Communications, Inc. © 1991. Used with permission from Billboard

BEST-SELLING NON-MOTION PICTURE HOME VIDEOS

Sports & Recreational

1. **Baseball Funnies**
   Simitar Entertainment
2. **Michael Jordon: Come Fly with Me**
   CBS-Fox Home Video
3. **Champions Forever**
   J2 Communications
4. **NBA Awesome Endings**
   CBS–Fox Home Video
5. **Not So Great Moments in Sports**
   HBO Home Video

Health & Fitness

1. **Callanetics**
   MCA/Universal Home Video
2. **Jane Fonda's Complete Workout**
   Warner Home Video
3. **Kathy Smith's Body Basics**
   JCI Video
4. **Kathy Smith's Fat-Burning Workout** *Fox Hills Video*
5. **Jane Fonda's Low Impact Aerobic Workout**
   Warner Home Video

Source: BPI Communications, Inc. © 1991. Used with permission from Billboard

MOM & POP & FLOP

If the faintest whisper of counter-culture entertainment exists in these "mass days," it's the rise of the cult video store, i.e., the kind of neighborhood spot that specializes in renting videotapes of the type of film shown on weeknights by drive-ins on the Jersey Shore in the '50s and '60s, like *Shanty Tramp*. In case you nodded off the first time you saw them on the big screen, you can rent them cheap and wonder why you went to see them in the first place.

SPORTS

THE MOST POPULAR SPECTATOR SPORTS IN AMERICA

Professional sports ranked by attendance

1.	**Baseball** *(major league)*	56,603,451
2.	**Thoroughbred racing**	56,194,565
3.	**Greyhound racing**	26,682,879
4.	**Harness racing**	18,560,871
5.	**Basketball** *(NBA)*	16,531,561
6.	**Football** *(NFL)*	15,725,662
7.	**Hockey** *(NHL)*	13,745,183
8.	**Auto racing**	11,207,481
9.	**Tennis**	7,503,339
10.	**Boxing**	6,407,432

Note: Horseracing figures include attendance at intertrack wagering outlets. Team sport figures include playoffs and championship events. To be fair, no one can say where boxing belongs on this list, but everyone agrees it's on there for sure. We do not consider professional wrestling a sport.

Source: The Daily Racing Form and league reports

Baseball and thoroughbred racing run neck and neck in the spectator sport sweepstakes.

PHOTOS: WIDE WORLD

BIG-TIME WINNERS
1990 Champions

National Football League: San Francisco 49ers (55–10 over the Denver Broncos)

National Basketball Association: Detroit Pistons (4–1 over the Portland Trailblazers)

National Hockey League: Edmonton Oilers (4–1 over the Boston Bruins)

Baseball World Series: Cincinnati Reds (4–0 over the Oakland Athletics)

Joe Montana

MOST POPULAR PARTICIPATION SPORTS

Sport	Participants* (in millions)
1. Swimming	70.5
2. Exercise walking	66.6
3. Bicycle riding	56.9
4. Fishing	46.5
4. Camping	46.5
6. Bowling	40.8
7. Exercise/equipment	31.5
8. Billiards/pool	29.6
9. Boating (motor)	29.0
10. Basketball	26.2

*Seven years of age and older
Source: National Sporting Goods Association

Super Bowl action.

Football's the game
MOST-WATCHED TELEVISED SPORTING EVENTS

Event	Network	Rating	Share
1. The Super Bowl XXIV	CBS	39.0	43
2. NFC Championship Game	CBS	26.4	46
3. AFC Championship Game	NBC	26.2	55
4. AFC Playoff Game (Sunday)	NBC	24.5	47
5. NFC Playoff Game (Sunday)	CBS	22.3	52
6. AFC Playoff Game (Sunday)	NBC	21.4	43
7. NCAA Basketball Championship	CBS	20.0	31
8. NFL Monday Night Football	ABC	19.9	34
9. NFL Monday Night Football	ABC	19.8	34
10. NFC Wild Card Game	CBS	19.7	46

Source: Nielsen Television Index Ranking Report

REDS STAR RISING

The 1990 World Series was not the greatest upset in baseball history, but it came as a nasty surprise to the Oakland Athletics when they suffered a 4-zip blowout at the hands of the Cincinnati Reds. Heavy hitting (22 runs to Oakland's 8) and ferocious pitching brought a sweet sweep to Reds skipper "Sweet Lou" Piniella—one of many managers cast aside by Yankee owner George Steinbrenner.

One other major league surprise: 9 no-hitters were thrown in 1990—the most since 1884.

SPORTS

HIGHEST-PAID ATHLETES

Buster Douglas

Athlete	Sport	Salary
1. Buster Douglas	Boxing	$19,558,000
2. Mike Tyson	Boxing	14,800,000
3. Evander Holyfield	Boxing	7,440,000
4. Patrick Ewing	Basketball	3,575,000
5. George Foreman	Boxing	3,025,000
6. Robin Yount	Baseball	3,200,000
7. Wayne Gretzky	Hockey	2,720,000
8. Kirby Puckett	Baseball	2,700,000
9. Charles Barkley	Basketball	2,600,000
9. Roger Clemens	Baseball	2,600,000

Note: Boxing figures equal 1990 purses minus managers' fees; others represent 1990 salary plus prorated share of signing bonus.
Source: Sport Magazine

Mike Tyson

Evander Holyfield

PHOTOS: WIDE WORLD

At one time, if you took the heavyweight boxers off this chart, you were left with only baseball players. No more. Basketball is coming on strong. There were several record-breaking contracts signed in 1990 for the 1991 season (and beyond): Baseball's Jose Canseco will get $33.5 million over 5 years but earn only $3.5 in 1991. Darryl Strawberry agreed to $20.25 million...$3.8 million of it in 1991. But for next year the biggest deal is for basketball star John "Hot Rod" Williams (left), who will collect $5 million from the Cleveland Cavaliers.

STAR-SPANGLED BLUNDER

The fat lady sang, but that was just the beginning, not the end: TV celeb Roseanne Barr's emetic torment of the national anthem at the July 25th San Diego Padres/Cincinnati Reds baseball game ranked as the year's premier publicity-stunt misfire. And when the startled crowd reacted predictably–with a chorus of boos–Ms. Barr countered with a crotch-grab that was more eloquent than her singing.

Barr's performance even drew a "tsk-tsk" from President Bush–himself a contender in the year's publicity-gaffe sweepstakes for his turnaround on taxes and his "read my hips" wisecrack.

TOP 10 SPORTS MONEY WINNERS

1990 Earnings

TENNIS

Men
1. Stefan Edberg — $1,995,901
2. Andre Agassi — 1,741,382
3. Boris Becker — 1,587,482
4. Ivan Lendl — 1,145,742
5. Pete Sampras — 900,057

Women
1. Steffi Graf — 1,921,863
2. Monica Seles — 1,637,222
3. Martina Navratilova — 1,330,794
4. Gabriela Sabatini — 975,490
5. Jana Novotna — 646,500

Source: Assoc. of Tennis Pros; Women's Tennis Assoc.

GOLF/PGA AND LPGA TOURS

Men
1. Greg Norman — $1,165,477
2. Wayne Levi — 1,024,647
3. Payne Stewart — 976,281
4. Paul Azinger — 944,731
5. Jodie Mudd — 911,746

Women
1. Beth Daniel — 863,578
2. Patty Sheehan — 732,618
3. Betsy King — 543,844
4. Cathy Gerring — 487,326
5. Pat Bradley — 480,018

Source: PGA Tour and LPGA

BOWLERS/PBA TOUR

1. Amieto Monacelli — $204,775
2. Chris Warren — 197,186
3. Parker Bohn III — 172,578
4. Ron Palombi, Jr. — 147,820
5. Brian Voss — 143,370
6. Jim Pencak — 136,770
7. Robert Lawrence — 131,880
8. Dave Husted — 128,840
9. Dave Ferraro — 111,968
10. Tony Westlake — 104,873

Source: Professional Bowlers Association

AUTO RACING NASCAR*

1. Dale Earnhardt — $3,083,056
2. Mark Martin — 1,302,958
3. Geoff Bodine — 1,131,222
4. Bill Elliott — 1,090,730
5. Rusty Wallace — 954,129
6. Ken Schrader — 769,934
7. Morgan Shepherd — 666,915
8. Ricky Rudd — 573,650
9. Alan Kulwicki — 550,936
10. Ernie Irvan — 535,280

*Final Winston Cup driver standings
Source: NASCAR

THOROUGHBRED RACING

1. Unbridled — $3,718,149
2. Izvestia — 2,486,667
3. Criminal Type — 2,270,290
4. In the Wings — 1,479,017
5. Bayakoa — 1,234,406
6. Summer Squall — 1,222,356
7. Ibn Bey — 1,132,414
8. Flying Continental — 1,096,700
9. Ruhlmann — 1,095,800
10. With Approval — 1,043,840

Source: Thoroughbred Racing Association; Daily Racing Form

STANDARDBRED RACING

1. Beach Towel — $2,091,860*
2. Jake and Elwood — 1,335,031
3. Artsplace — 1,180,271
4. Apache's Fame — 1,157,731
5. Die Laughing — 1,142,322
6. Miss Easy — 1,128,956
7. Harmonious — 1,033,942
8. Embassy Lobell — 1,005,175
9. Dorunrun Bluegrass — 851,755
10. Topnotcher — 800,501

*New single-season record
Source: Harness Tracks of America, Inc.

A BAD DAY AT THE RACES

For racehorses, this was a black year: Studs Northern Dancer and Alydar died, and worst of all was the loss of Go For Wand, a winning filly who snapped her leg (and was then humanely destroyed) while running head to head with Bayakoa in one of the Breeders' Cup Sprints at Belmont Park, NY, in October. Same day, same track, later race: Mr. Nickerson suffered "severe acute pulmonary hemorrhage," i.e., bleeding into the lungs, then leaped into the air and fell dead. Shaker Knit fell over Mr. Nickerson and suffered irreparable damage to the spine and was humanely destroyed. All this before a shocked crowd at a very popular race.

Go For Wand goes down.

SPORTS

TOP-RANKED COLLEGE BASKETBALL TEAMS
Final UPI Board of Coaches ratings

School	Record	Rating
1. Oklahoma	26 - 4	586
2. Nevada-Las Vegas	29 - 5	520
3. Connecticut	28 - 5	510
4. Michigan State	26 - 5	457
5. Kansas	29 - 4	368
6. Syracuse	24 - 6	340
7. Georgia Tech	24 - 6	296
8. Arkansas	26 - 4	282
9. Georgetown	23 - 6	264
10. Purdue	21 - 7	222

Source: United Press International

TOP-RANKED COLLEGE FOOTBALL TEAMS
Final UPI Board of Coaches ratings

School	Record	Rating
1. Georgia Tech	11 - 0 - 1	847
2. Colorado	11 - 1 - 1	846
3. Miami	10 - 2	763
4. Florida State	10 - 2	677
5. Washington	10 - 2	664
6. Notre Dame	9 - 3	548
7. Tennessee	9 - 2 - 2	449
8. Michigan	9 - 3	426
9. Clemson	10 - 2	420
10. Penn State	9 - 3	301

Source: United Press International

SAY "GOODBYE," GEORGE

George Steinbrenner, who for 17 years made "Yankee fan" a synonym for "mixed feelings," surprised everyone—not by dealing too sharply for his own good with gambler Howie Spira (GS had, after all, been chastised by three baseball commissioners a total of nine times), but by dealing himself right out of the game.

BLOOM OFF ROSE

Pete Rose, baseball's leading hitter, brought new meaning to his nickname, "Mr. Hustle," and acquired a new record (prison) in 1990. No, he didn't go to Cooperstown (he was eligible this year for the Hall of Fame); he went to the federal prison at Marion, IL, to serve a five-month term for income-tax evasion.

Stat Wrap

BASEBALL **BATTING AVERAGES**

National League
1. Willie McGee .335
2. Eddie Murray .330
3. Dave Magadan .328
4. Len Dykstra .325
5. Andre Dawson .310

American League
1. George Brett .329
2. Rickey Henderson .325
3. Rafael Palmeiro .319
4. Alan Trammell .304
5. Wade Boggs .302

Source: National and American Leagues of Professional Baseball Clubs

BASEBALL **EARNED RUN AVERAGES**

National League
1. Danny Darwin 2.21
2. Zane Smith 2.55
3. Ed Whitson 2.60
4. Frank Viola 2.67
5. Jose Rijo 2.70

American League
1. Roger Clemens 1.93
2. Chuck Finley 2.40
3. Dave Stewart 2.56
4. Kevin Appier 2.76
5. Dave Stieb 2.93

Source: National and American Leagues of Professional Baseball Clubs

FOOTBALL **TOTAL YARDS RUSHING**

1. Barry Sanders 1304
2. Thurman Thomas 1297
3. Marion Butts 1225
4. Earnest Byner 1219
5. Bobby Humphrey 1202
6. Neal Anderson 1078
7. Barry Word 1015
8. James Brooks 1004
9. Randall Cunningham 942
10. Emmitt Smith 937

Source: National Football League

FOOTBALL **QUARTERBACK EFFICIENCY**

1. Jim Kelly 101.2
2. Warren Moon 96.8
3. Steve DeBerg 96.3
4. Phil Simms 92.7
5. Randall Cunningham 91.6
6. Jay Schroeder 90.8
7. Joe Montana 89.0
8. Dan Marino 82.6
9. Jim Harbaugh 81.9
10. Bubby Brister 81.6

Source: National Football League

BASKETBALL **SCORING AVERAGES***

1. Michael Jordan 33.5
2. Karl Malone 31.0
3. Patrick Ewing 28.5
4. Tom Chambers 27.2
5. Dominique Wilkins 26.7
6. Charles Barkley 25.2
7. Chris Mullin 25.1
8. Reggie Miller 24.6
9. Akeem Olajuwon 24.3
9. David Robinson 24.3

* Per game
Source: National Basketball Association

BASKETBALL **REBOUNDING AVERAGES***

1. Akeem Olajuwon 14.0
2. David Robinson 12.0
3. Charles Barkley 11.5
4. Karl Malone 11.1
5. Patrick Ewing 10.9
6. Rony Seikaly 10.4
7. Robert Parish 10.1
8. Moses Malone 10.0
8. Michael Cage 10.0
10. Buck Williams 9.8

* Per game
Source: National Basketball Association

GENDER FLAP

When Lisa Olson, sportswriter for the Boston *Herald,* was interrupted during a September post-practice locker room interview by five naked Patriots including tight end Zeke Mowatt spouting lewd remarks and invitations, the long-dormant issue of women reporters covering men's sports sprang back to life. By the time coaches, players and sports-media types (male and female) put the issue to rest, Mowatt was fined $2,000, Olson was a talk-show celeb, and Patriots owner and Remington-shaver magnate Victor Kiam had dropped $100,000 in a public-relations fumble.

Lisa Olson in the Patriots' locker room.

LEISURE TIME

A report published in 1990 by the Roper Organization surveyed Americans' leisure-time interests. Respondents were asked to rate specific activities according to degree of interest.

MOST-PREFERRED LEISURE-TIME PURSUITS

Ranked by percent of respondents who claimed to be "very interested" or "moderately interested" in the options listed.*

Interest	Percent
1. Television	86%
2. Movies	73
3. Popular music	70
3. Travel (in U.S.)	70
5. Cooking	60
6. Professional sports	55
7. Reading (novels)	51
8. Reading (nonfiction)	48
8. Theater	48
10. Participation sports	46

*See note 4, page 90, for complete list

MOST-PREFERRED HOBBIES AND ACTIVITIES

Ranked by percent of respondents who characterized the listed** options as a "real hobby" or "interest"...to quote the survey, something "you actually do or engage in yourself."

Activity	Percent
1. Reading	43%
2. Cooking	34
3. Music	32
4. Gardening	26
5. Pets	25
6. Fishing	24
7. Swimming	20
7. Travel	20
9. Camping	18
10. Crafts	17

**See note 4, page 90, for complete list

Source (both charts): Roper Reports, a syndicated research service of The Roper Organization, New York

POTATODOM

The clear winner of Americans' leisure-time attention is television. Staring at the electronic window consumes 15 hours a week or 40% of our leisure hours, and that number is growing: the more time we have, the more time we spend on TV. Men watch more than women; the less you work the more you watch; and the more education you have, the less you watch. Sunday is the big day.

Source: American Demographics

MOST POPULAR FORMS OF GAMBLING

Form of Gambling	Total Wagered ($ millions)
1. Casinos	$195,962
2. Sports (illegal)	27,387
3. Lotteries	19,468
4. Horse books (illegal)	8,128
5. Numbers (illegal)	5,550
6. Non-bingo charitable games	3,990
7. Cardrooms	3,798
8. Bingo	3,772
9. Greyhounds	3,211
10. Legal books	1,434

Source: Gaming & Wagering Business

MOST EFFICIENT FORMS OF EXERCISE

Ranked by calories burned per hour by a 150-pound man

Activity	Calories Burned
1. Cross-country skiing	1,100
2. Running (not jogging)	900
3. Bicycling (stationary)	850
4. Bicycling (13 mph)	660
5. Swimming	650
6. Rowing machine	600
6. Tennis	600
8. Handball/racquetball	570
9. Jogging (13-min. mile)	565
10. Aerobics	530

Source: Compiled for Top 10 by John E. Barrett

CHAIRMAN OF THE BOARDS

Monopoly still has a lock on board-game popularity in America. Thousands of wannabes have come and gone since 1935, when Charles B. Darrow of Germantown, PA, launched the now familiar tabletop arena of real estate speculation. Parker Brothers went on to sell over 100 million sets worldwide (the game is translated into 23 languages, including Russian, and marketed in 80 countries).

It's a participatory soap opera—a first-hand chance to indulge in greed, conspiracy, double-crossing, cheating and exploitation.

No wonder it's so popular.

BUSINESS

LARGEST U.S. INDUSTRIAL CORPORATIONS

From the Fortune 500

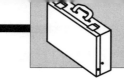

Company	Location	Sales ($ millions)
1. General Motors	Detroit, MI	$126,974
2. Ford Motor Company	Dearborn, MI	96,933
3. Exxon	New York, NY	86,656
4. IBM	Armonk, NY	63,438
5. General Electric	Fairfield, CT	55,264
6. Mobil Oil	New York, NY	50,976
7. Philip Morris	New York, NY	39,069
8. Chrysler Motors	Highland Park, MI	36,156
9. E.I. Du Pont de Nemours	Wilmington, DL	35,209
10. Texaco	White Plains, NY	32,416

LARGEST U.S. SERVICE CORPORATIONS

From the Fortune Service 500

Company	Location	Sales ($ millions)
1. AT&T	New York, NY	$36,345
2. Fleming Cos.	Oklahoma City, OK	12,045
3. Super Valu Stores	Eden Prairie, MI	10,316
4. Enron	Houston, TX	9,870
5. Marriott	Bethesda, MD	8,382
6. United Telecom.	Westwood, KA	7,549
7. McKesson	San Francisco, CA	7,515
8. American Financial	Cincinnati, OH	7,286
9. Sysco	Houston, TX	6,851
10. Pacific Enterprises	Los Angeles, CA	6,797

Source (both charts): Reprinted by permission from Fortune Magazine; ©1990 The Time Inc. Magazine Company

BIG DEALS

The highest-paid entertainers ranked according to total combined estimated income for 1989 and 1990 (in millions, of course).

Mr. Cosby

Talent	2-Year Total	1990
1. Bill Cosby	$115	$55
2. Michael Jackson	100	35
3. Rolling Stones	88	44
4. Steven Spielberg	87	23
5. New Kids on the Block	78	61
6. Oprah Winfrey	68	38
7. Sylvester Stallone	63	25
8. Madonna	62	39
9. Arnold Schwarzenegger	55	20
10. Charles M. Schulz	54	26

Source: Excerpted with permission of Forbes magazine, October 1, 1990. © Forbes Inc. 1990

AMERICAN BILLIONAIRES
Ranked by family wealth

Name/Age	Wealth ($ billions)	Source
1. Forrest E. Mars, Sr., 86 Forrest E. Mars, Jr., 59 John F. Mars, 54 Jacqueline Mars Vogel, 50	$12.5	Candy bars
2. Samuel I. Newhouse, 62, and family Donald E. Newhouse, 60, and family	11.5	Publishing
3. Sam Moore Walton, 72	7.3	Discount retailing
4. John Werner Kluge, 75	7.0	Media properties
5. Charles Koch, 54 David Koch, 50	4.7	Oil
6. Anne Cox Chambers, 70 Barbara Cox Anthony, 67	4.5	Media properties
6. Perry Bass, 76 Sid Richardson Bass, 47 Edward Perry Bass, 45 Robert Muse Bass, 42 Lee Marshall Bass, 33	4.5	Oil, real estate, equity investments
6. Jay Pritzker, 68 Robert Pritzker, 64	4.5	Hotels
9. Eugene Paul Getty (J. Paul Jr.), 58 Gordon Peter Getty, 56	3.8	Oil
9. Mary Idema Pew, 63 Robert Pew, 66 Robert Pew, Jr., 39 Kate Pew Wolters, 33	3.8	Office furniture, real estate
9. Warren Edward Buffett, 60	3.8	Investments

Source: Reprinted by permission from Fortune Magazine; ©1990 The Time Inc. Magazine Company

LARGEST JUNK BOND DEFAULTS
Ranking the year's big bankruptcies

Company	Face Amount Outstanding ($ millions)	Company	Face Amount Outstanding ($ millions)
1. Allied/Federated Dept. Stores	$1,706	6. Linter Textiles	$200
2. Southland	1,252	7. Leaseway Transport	193
3. Western Union	500	8. General Development	175
4. Gillett Holdings	421	9. Greyhound Lines	150
5. Ames Dept. Stores	200	10. Service America	127

Source: The Bear Truth investment newsletter

PACIFIC MERGER

It's the biggest American anything sold to Japanese owners for the biggest price paid for anything in 1990: MCA, owner of Universal Pictures, Universal Studios Theme Park, Geffen Records, MCA Television, and thousands of old Universal pictures, including *E.T.* and *Jaws*. Hollywood studios have become fiscal black holes, and Matsushita Electrical Industrial Co. (makers of popular Panasonic, Technics, Quasar brands of electronic entertainment gear) had something like $12 billion in the bank, and under-chairman Akio Tanii, a hankering to match rival Sony (new owner of Columbia Pictures) and to get control of entertainment "software" to match its hardware.

BUSINESS

Beatrice products.

LARGEST BLACK ENTERPRISES

From the Black Enterprise 100

Company	Location	Sales ($ millions)
1. TLC Beatrice Intl.	New York, NY	$1,514,000
2. Johnson Publishing Co.	Chicago, IL	241,327
3. Philadelphia Coca-Cola	Philadelphia, PA	240,000
4. H.J. Russell & Co.	Atlanta, GA	132,876
5. The Gordy Co.	Los Angeles, CA	100,000
6. Soft Sheen Products Inc.	Chicago, Il	87,200
7. Trans Jones Inc.	Monroe, MI	78,555
8. The Bing Group	Detroit, MI	73,883
9. The Maxima Corp.	Rockville, MD	58,383
10. Dick Griffey Productions	Hollywood, CA	50,162

Source: The Earl G. Graves Publishing Co., Inc., © June 1990. All rights reserved

FASTEST-GROWING SMALL PRIVATE COMPANIES

From the Inc. 500

Company	Location	Business	Percent Sales Growth
1. Cogentrix	Charlotte, NC	Cogeneration facilities	151,681%
2. Gateway 2000	N. Sioux City, SD	Makes and sells PCs	69,775
3. CEBCOR	Chicago, IL	Employee leasing	39,636
4. Corporate Express	Aurora, CO	Dist. office products	24,644
5. ComputerWare	Palo Alto, CA	Sells hardware/software	21,916
6. LGB	Chula Vista, CA	Makes swimwear	13,349
7. Brookfree	San Diego, CA	Computer components	17,244
8. ATC Services	Atlanta, GA	Temporary medical help	15,044
9. Octocom Systems	Wilmington, MA	Makes data comm. systs.	14,866
10. Northgate Computer Systems	Eden Prairie, MN	Makes and sells PCs	13,555

Source: Reprinted with permission of Inc. Magazine. © 1990 by Goldhirsh Group

THE GREATEST TREASURY RAID

As the savings & loan losses continue to mount, the hits just keep on coming. During 1990, the red ink amounted to $500 billion, which of course is to be paid by taxpayers. Highlights: Neil Bush, the President's son, was chastised for his role in the questionable loans that sank Silverado Savings, one of Colorado's largest failures. And the biggest bust of them all–Charles Keating's Lincoln Savings and Loan–effectively smirched the careers of five U.S. Senators who accepted a total of $1.3 million in campaign contributions and other donations from Keating and who in various ways intervened with government regulators and examiners on his behalf.

Neil Bush

MOST VALUABLE CORPORATIONS

Ranked by market value of stock as of December 31, 1990

Company	Market Value ($ billions)	Last Year's Rank
1. Exxon	$64.2	2
2. IBM	63.8	1
3. General Electric	50.2	3
4. Philip Morris	47.9	5
5. Bristol Myers - Squibb	35.2	8
6. Merck	35.1	7
7. Wal-Mart	34.3	11
8. AT&T	32.8	4
9. Procter & Gamble	30.1	17
10. Coca-Cola	29.8	15

Note: General Motors, in sixth place last year, is off the list for the first time.
Source: Stock market reports

The Exxon Valdez.

PHOTO: WIDE WORLD

HIGHEST-PAID CHIEF EXECUTIVES

Name	Company	Total Compensation ($ thousands)
1. Craig O. McCaw	McCaw Cellular	$53,944
2. Steven J. Ross	Time Warner	34,200
3. Donald A. Pels	Lin Broadcasting	22,791
4. Jim P. Manzi	Lotus Development	16,363
5. Paul Fireman	Reebok International	14,606
6. Ronald K. Richey	Torchmark	12,666
7. Martin S. Davis	Paramount	11,635
8. Roberto C. Goizueta	Coca-Cola	10,715
9. Michael D. Eisner	Walt Disney	9,589
10. August A. Busch III	Anheuser-Busch	8,861

Source: Reprinted from the article "Top 20 Highest-Paid Chief Executive Officers" from the May 7, 1990 issue of Business Week by special permission. © 1990 by McGraw-Hill, Inc.

The Donald

PHOTO: WIDE WORLD

THE ART OF THE FALL

Donald Trump, who in earlier years seemed to fly as high as the New York air shuttle that bore his name, spent much of 1990 verifying the old wheeze about "what goes up..." Items: his over-leveraged Taj Mahal failed to bring in enough moolah to service its debt; Ivana filed for divorce, declined to abide by their prenuptial agreement, and said "See you in court"; and his heavily promoted second book, *Surviving at the Top*, did not.

Sic transit, etc.

BUSINESS

LARGEST INDUSTRIES
By employment

Industry	Total Employment (in thousands)
1. Health services	8,122
2. Eating & drinking places	6,503
3. Business services	5,898
4. Durable goods	3,759
5. Transportaion	3,665
6. Food stores	3,379
7. Finance	3,363
8. Nondurable goods	2,595
9. Gen'l merchandise stores	2,435
10. Insurance	2,165

Source: U.S. Dept. of Labor

LARGEST U.S. EXPORTERS

Company	Product	Export Sales ($ millions)
1. Boeing	Commercial and military aircraft	$11,021
2. General Motors	Motor vehicles and parts	10,185
3. Ford Motor	Motor vehicles and parts	8,602
4. General Electric	Jet engines, turbines, medical systems	7,268
5. IBM	Computers and related equipment	5,476
6. Du Pont	Specialty chemicals	4,844
7. Chrysler	Motor vehicles and parts	4,649
8. United Technologies	Jet engines, helicopters, cooling equip.	3,307
9. Caterpillar	Heavy machinery, engines, turbines	3,291
10. McDonnell Douglas	Commercial and military aircraft	2,896

Source: The Bear Truth investment newsletter

THE WHOLE WORLD'S A STAGE...AND AN AUDIENCE

Entertainment media are America's number two export (after aircraft). The world watches our films, listens to our recorded music, minds our sports spectacles, absorbs our television productions, and even watches our plays and reads our books–more than those of any other single culture. In a time of doubts about military and economic might, America is emerging as the world's lone popular-entertainment superpower.

How big a business is American show business? According to a 1990 article in *Time* magazine, U.S. entertainment product captures the lion's share of world revenues in almost every medium.

Medium	Percentage
Television	75%
Pay television	85
Motion pictures	55
Home video	55
Recorded music	50
Books	35

ECONOMIC INDICATORS

Indicator	Basis	1990	1989
1. Consumer Price Index	Annual	5.5%	4.8%
2. Unemployment	Year-end	5.8%	5.3%
3. GNP growth	Annual	1.0%*	2.5%
4. Money supply growth (M2)	Annual	3.4%	4.9%
5. Treasury bills (6 mo.)	Year-end	6.89%	8.06%
6. CDs (6 mo.)	Year-end	7.47%	7.59%
7. Mortgage (30 yr. fixed)	Year-end	9.64%	9.75%
8. Trade deficit (in billions)	Annual	$110.7	$110.0
9. New housing starts (in millions)	Annual	1.21	1.40
10. Auto production (in millions)	Annual	6.3	6.8

*Estimated
Source: Compiled for Top 10 by The Bear Truth investment newsletter

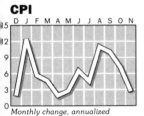

CPI — Monthly change, annualized

UNEMPLOYMENT — Month-end survey

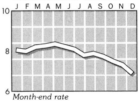

TREASURY BILLS — Month-end rate

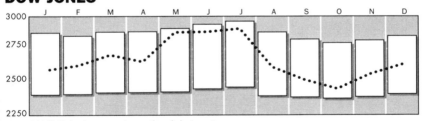

DOW JONES

••• Dotted rule represents month-end closing price

A YEAR TO FORGET
Return on investments: 1990

1. One-year CD	7.9%
2. Money-market funds	7.8
3. Old master paintings	7.7
4. U.S. Government bond funds	6.0
5. Private homes	-1.9
6. Gold bullion	-2.4
7. U.S. growth funds	-5.5
8. Junk-bond funds	-11.9
9. International stock funds	-12.8
10. Gold funds	-24.8

Old masters did about as well as anything.

7.7%

BUSINESS

BIGGEST BUSINESS DEALS
Completed in 1990

	Company	Target	Type of Transaction	Value* ($ billions)
1.	Time, Inc.	Warner Communications Inc.	Acquisition	$14.10
2.	Matsushita	MCA Inc.	Acquisition	5.59
3.	McCaw Cellular	LIN Broadcasting Corp.	Acquisition	3.99
4.	Philip Morris	Jacobs Suchard AG	Acquisition	3.83
5.	Georgia-Pacific	Great Northern Nekoosa Corp.	Acquisition	3.60
6.	IMA Holdings	American Medical Int. Inc.	Leveraged buyout	3.31
7.	ConAgra Inc.	Beatrice Cos.	Divestiture	3.29
8.	Accor SA	Motel 6 LT	Merger	2.30
9.	Bass PLC	Holiday Inn, Inc.	Merger	2.23
10.	Sovren Financial	Citizens and Southern Corp.	Merger	2.05

*Includes assumption of refinancing of debt. Source: Securities Data Company

The cover of Time Warner's first annual report. **WHY?**

The Big Board's **BEST-PERFORMING STOCKS**

	Common Stock	Closing Price	Percent Change from '89
1.	Cabletron Systems	28 1/2	204.0%
2.	US Surgical	71 3/8	160.7
3.	Signal Apparel	10 1/2	147.1
4.	EMC Corp.	8	146.2
5.	Foxboro Co.	51 7/8	126.8
6.	LE Meyers Group	15 1/8	124.1
7.	Oregon Steel Mills	24	97.9
8.	Clayton Homes	13 3/4	96.4
9.	International Rectifier	11	91.3
10.	Fabri-Centers of America	25 3/4	87.3

Source: The New York Stock Exchange

THE JUNKMAN GOETH

Directly to Jail, it turns out. Michael Milken, the Drexel Burnham Lambert financial guru who championed the junk-bond concept and white-collar greed, will now spend the next decade behind bars. In late November, U.S. District Judge Kimba Wood sentenced Milken to 10 years in prison and 3 years of community service for his part in the ongoing Wall Street insider-trading scandals.

Earlier convictions had brought large fines but jail sentences more appropriate for stealing car radios than investors' millions. Milken, however, had become a powerful symbol of crooked Wall Street sharpies.

Michael Milken leaving U.S. District Court in Manhattan.

ADVERTISING

BIGGEST-SPENDING NATIONAL ADVERTISERS

Company	Location	Total U.S. Spending ($ millions)
1. Philip Morris Cos.	New York, NY	$2,072
2. Procter & Gamble Co.	Cincinnati, OH	1,779
3. Sears, Roebuck & Co.	Chicago, IL	1,432
4. General Motors Corp	Detroit, MI	1,364
5. Grand Metropolitan PLC	London	823
6. PepsiCo Inc.	Purchase, NY	786
7. McDonald's Corp.	Oak Brook, IL	774
8. Eastman Kodak Co.	Rochester, NY	719
9. RJR Nabisco	New York, NY	704
10. Kellogg Co.	Battle Creek, MI	612

Products of the Philip Morris Companies.

NATIONAL AD SPENDING *Ranked by category*

Category	Total U.S. Spending ($ millions)	Category	Total U.S. Spending ($ millions)
1. Retail	$6,029	6. Toiletries, cosmetics	2,212
2. Automotive	5,520	7. Travel, hotels	2,133
3. Food	3,898	8. Drugs, remedies	1,605
4. Services (business & consumer)	3,891	9. Beer, wine, liquor	1,185
5. Entertainment	2,753	10. Direct-response cosmetics	1,151

Source (both charts): Reprinted with permission from the March 26, 1990 issue of Advertising Age. © Crain Communications Inc., 1990

STATUS SNEAKER

Nike Air Jordans

The prices of sneakers like Nike Air Jordans ($125) and Reebok Pumps ($130) soared over the $100 barrier with unforeseen side effects: just wearing them in some city neighborhoods could get you mugged or even killed. As if the sneaker/violence link-up weren't image problem enough, Jesse Jackson's Operation PUSH challenged Nike to recycle some of the estimated millions it was reaping from black buyers by purchasing from black suppliers and hiring more blacks. Meeting resistance, PUSH instituted a black-community boycott of Nike products in July. The boycott may not have hurt Air Jordan sales, but Nike has named a black to its board and hired a minority-owned advertising agency.

ADVERTISING

LARGEST ADVERTISING AGENCIES

U.S. agencies ranked by worldwide gross income

Agency	Headquarters	Gross Income ($ millions)
1. Saatchi & Saatchi	New York	$890
2. Young & Rubicam	New York	865
3. Backer Spielvogel Bates	New York	760
4. McCann-Erickson	New York	716
5. Ogilvy and Mather	New York	700
6. BBDO	New York	657
7. J. Walter Thompson	New York	626
8. Lintas	New York	593
9. DDB Needham	New York	553
10. Foote, Cone & Belding	Chicago	511

Source: Reprinted with permission from the March 26, 1990 issue of Advertising Age. © Crain Communications Inc., 1990

TOP MEGA-BRAND ADVERTISERS

Ranked by first-half 1990 ad spending

Company	($ thousands)
1. AT&T	$253,460
2. McDonald's restaurants	217,202
3. Sears stores	212,730
4. Kellogg breakfast foods	205,549
5. Ford cars and trucks	176,400
6. Toyota cars and trucks	126,708
7. Kraft foods	125,162
8. Chevrolet cars	124,054
9. Nissan cars and trucks	115,324
10. Pepsi beverages	85,605

Source: Reprinted with permission from the November 19, 1990 issue of Advertising Age. © Crain Communications Inc., 1990

BIGFOOT IN MOUTH

Volvo builds a tough car, but when its advertising agency–Scali, McCabe, Sloves Inc.–built a campaign around the car's resistance to getting flattened by one of those monster-wheel pickups in a U.S. Hot Rod Association event, what they got was a very tough time. The Texas attorney general learned that the Volvo had been reinforced and the other vehicles weakened–facts that were not disclosed to the public. When Texas sued, Volvo apologized and paid a $300,000 fine. Scali, McCabe resigned the $43 million account.

LEADING MEDIA COMPANIES
Ranked by revenue

Company	Location	Revenue ($ millions)
1. Capital Cities/ABC	New York, NY	$4,767
2. Time Warner	New York, NY	4,575
3. Gannett Co.	Arlington, VA	3,518
4. General Electric	Fairfield, CT	3,392
5. CBS, Inc.	New York, NY	2,960
6. Advance Publications	Newark, NJ	2,882
7. Times Mirror Corp.	Los Angeles, CA	2,807
8. TCI	Denver, CO	2,353
9. Knight-Rider	Miami, FL	2,262
10. Tribune Co.	Chicago, IL	2,095

Source: Reprinted from the June 25, 1990 issue of Advertising Age. © 1991 Crain Communications Inc.

Capital Cities/ABC world headquarters.

NATIONAL AD SPENDING
Ranked by media

Media	Total U.S. Spending ($ millions)
1. Network TV	$7249
2. Spot TV	3,664
3. Magazine	2,901
4. Newspaper	2,077
5. Syndicated TV	942
6. Spot radio	717
7. Cable-TV networks	518
8. Network radio	431
9. Outdoor	276
10. Sunday magazine	236

Source: Reprinted from the March 26, 1990 issue of Advertising Age. © 1991 Crain Communications Inc.

THE CAMEL IN THE CLASSROOM

Like the nose of a camel entering a tent, Whittle Communications' controversial Channel One television news program moved from suggestion to reality in 1990. By year's end, Whittle had contracts with some 6,000 schools nationwide, reaching an audience of about 4 million teen-agers. The schools get a "package" of color TV sets for classrooms, 2 VCRs and a satellite dish (worth an estimated $50,000). Whittle gets a captive audience for its 12-minute, professionally prepared daily news program specifically targeted to teens, including 2 minutes of commercial messages (e.g., Burger King, Clearasil, Snickers) for which advertisers are charged hundreds of thousands of dollars. Students get the news–plus a real-life lesson about free lunch.

TECHNOLOGY

LARGEST HIGH-TECHNOLOGY COMPANIES

Company	Location	Sales ($ millions)
1. IBM	Armonk, NY	$63,438
2. Boeing	Seattle, WA	20,276
3. United Technologies	Hartford, CT	19,766
4. Xerox	Stamford, CT	17,635
5. McDonnell Douglas	St. Louis, MO	14,995
6. Digital Equipment	Maynard, MA	12,866
7. Rockwell International	El Segundo, CA	12,633
8. Hewlett-Packard	Palo Alto, CA	11,899
9. Unisys	Blue Bell, PA	10,097
10. General Dynamics	St. Louis, MO	10,053

Source: Company reports

BEST-SELLING HOME ELECTRONICS

Product	Sales ($ millions)
1. Color TV receivers	$6,530
2. Videocassette recorders	4,632
3. Auto sound equipment	4,125
4. Separate audio components	1,871
5. Portable audio tape equip.	1,595
6. Audio systems	1,217
7. Accessories	1,001
8. Blank videocassettes	923
9. Projection TV	478
10. Home radio	379

Source: U.S. Consumer Electronics Industry Assoc.

The bulk of the billions at left are going to Japan. Now they're working on the billions in the chart above.

ON THE COSTS OF THE B-2 BOMBER PROGRAM

You'd be nervous parallel-parking a $60,000 Mercedes? How do you think U.S. Air Force pilots feel about landing a B-2 bomber at over $500 million apiece? (And that's only if the Department of Defense buys the full order of 132 aircraft; if fewer are purchased from builder Northrop, the costs go even higher.) These are the most expensive weapons systems, in the history of the country. What do B-2s do? Well, they carry bombs, of course, plus three crewpersons. And, designated as "stealth" aircraft, they sneak fast. No word on how tricky they are to land.

Will the war in the Gulf affect the fortunes of the B-2? Stay tuned.

BEST-SELLING PERSONAL COMPUTERS

	Company/Computer	Market Share
1.	IBM PS/2-55SX	10%
2.	IBM PS/2-50Z	9
3.	IBM PS/2-70	8
4.	IBM PS/2-30 286	4
4.	Compaq Deskpro 386	4
6.	IBM PS/2-30	3
6.	Apple Macintosh SE	3
8.	Zenith 2248	3
9.	Apple Macintosh-II CX	2
9.	Apple Macintosh II	2

Source: Computer Intelligence, ADAPSO Market Trends 1990

Note: both these charts are based on a survey of 1,500 businesses with 500 or more employees.

IBM PS/2-55SX

BEST-SELLING PERSONAL COMPUTER SOFTWARE

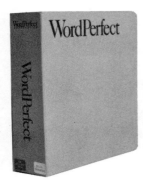

	Company/Program	Market Share
1.	WordPerfect/WordPerfect	23%
2.	Lotus/1-2-3	21
3.	Microsoft/Word	8
4.	Microsoft/Excel	4
5.	SPC/Harvard Graphics	3
5.	Borland Quattro/Quattro-Pro	3
5.	IBM/DisplayWrite	3
8.	Ashton-Tate/MultiMate	2
8.	Ashton-Tate/dBase IV	2
8.	Ashton-Tate/dBase III/III+	2

Source: Computer Intelligence, Intelligence Report

HUBBLE TROUBLE

Farthest-out snafu of the year came to light when the amply hyped Hubble Space Telescope achieved orbit in June. Instead of providing our sharpest-ever looks at deep space, everything looked kind of...fuzzy. Turned out the primary mirror was perfectly ground to the wrong shape by NASA contractor Perkin-Elmer Corporation; P-E actually detected the error in a quality-control test, but decided that the test itself must be wrong, so up she went.

Devices to improve its vision will be shuttled up to Hubble in the next few years, but in the meantime NASA is orbiting a glass paperweight that cost an astronomical $1.5 billion.

ATTRACTIONS

MOST POPULAR THEME & AMUSEMENT PARKS

Park	Location	Attendance
1. **Walt Disney World** (Includes The Magic Kingdom, EPCOT & Disney-MGM Studios)	Lake Buena Vista, FL	28,500,000
2. **Disneyland**	Anaheim, CA	12,900,000
3. **Knott's Berry Farm**	Buena Park, CA	5,000,000
4. **Universal Studios Hollywood**	Universal City, CA	4,625,000
5. **Sea World of Florida**	Orlando, FL	3,800,000
6. **Sea World of California**	San Diego, CA	3,282,040
7. **Kings Island**	Kings Island, OH	3,209,777
8. **Six Flags Magic Mountain**	Valencia, CA	3,100,000
9. **Cedar Point**	Sandusky, OH	3,087,000
10. **Busch Gardens, The Dark Continent**	Tampa, FL	3,050,000

Source: Amusement Business Magazine

PHOTO: © 1991 KNOTT'S BERRY FARM

PHOTO: © 1990 UNIVERSAL CITY STUDIOS, INC.

Pictured far left: the new Boomerang coaster at Knott's Berry Farm, the #3 park. Left: the wildly popular Kongfrontation at #4 Universal Studios Hollywood. The folks at Disney (#1 & #2) wouldn't come up with a picture for us.

KING KONG KO

Billed as a worthy rival to Disney World, Orlando's other attraction, the new $630 million Universal Studios Florida demonstrated the universal reach of Murphy's Law: from King Kong on down, nothing roared or quaked quite as planned. On the hurried-up June 7 opening day, most of the 13 major attractions, including E.T. (the ride), Kongfrontation and Earthquake, malfunctioned. It was the paying customers who did the howling—for their money back. Management blamed it on computer software and responded with a two-for-one ticket deal.

ILLUSTRATION: DAVID VOGLER

MOST POPULAR ZOOS

Zoo	Location	Attendance
1. Lincoln Park Zoo	Chicago, IL	4,300,000
2. San Diego Zoo	San Diego, CA	3,300,000
3. National Zoo	Washington, D.C.	3,000,000
3. Busch Gardens	Tampa, FL	3,000,000
5. St. Louis Zoo	St. Louis, MO	2,750,000
6. New York Zoological Park (Bronx Zoo)	New York, NY	2,500,000
7. Los Angeles Zoo	Los Angeles, CA	2,000,000
8. Chicago Zoological Park (Brookfield Zoo)	Chicago, IL	1,950,000
9. Milwaukee County Zoo	Milwaukee, WI	1,700,000
10. Philadelphia Zoo	Philadelphia, PA	1,300,000

Pictured above: Koundu, a gorilla from the Lincoln Park Zoo. At right: Shamu, a killer whale performing at Sea World of Florida.

MOST POPULAR AQUARIUMS

Aquarium	Location	Attendance
1. Sea World of Florida	Orlando, FL	4,000,000
2. Sea World of California	San Diego, CA	3,700,000
3. Sea World of Texas	San Antonio, TX	2,500,000
4. Monterey Bay Aquarium	Monterey, CA	1,700,000
5. National Aquarium	Baltimore, MD	1,500,000
6. Marine World Africa USA	Vallejo, CA	1,410,000
7. Sea World of Ohio	Aurora, OH	1,300,000
8. New England Aquarium	Boston, MA	1,200,000
9. John G. Shedd Aquarium	Chicago, IL	1,000,000
10. Mystic Marinelife Aquarium	Mystic, CT	760,000

Source (both charts): American Association of Zoological Parks and Aquariums

THE CINCINNATI KISS

The photographs of the late Robert Mapplethorpe have been generating controversy ever since they hit the traveling exhibit trail, especially where funded by federal government grants. The legal issue of what lies in the eye of the beholder—art, beauty, smut, whatever—was joined when a local grand jury indicted Dennis Barrie, director of Cincinnati's Contemporary Arts Center, on criminal obscenity charges. Barrie was acquitted on October 5. Side effects: prices of Mapplethorpe pix skyrocketed, attendance quadrupled, membership increased by 80%. Trial cost much more than the original $30,000 National Endowment for the Arts grant with its odious and almost certainly unconstitutional obscenity clause.

Dennis Barrie

ATTRACTIONS

MOST POPULAR NATIONAL PARKS

	National Park	Location	Attendance
1.	Great Smoky Mountains	N. Carolina & Tennessee	8,333,600
2.	Acadia	Maine	5,441,000
3.	Grand Canyon	Arizona	3,966,200
4.	Yosemite	California	3,308,200
5.	Olympic	Washington	2,737,600
6.	Yellowstone	Wyoming	2,644,400
7.	Rocky Mountain	Colorado	2,502,900
8.	Zion	Utah	1,998,900
9.	Shenandoah	Virginia	1,873,800
10.	Glacier	Montana	1,821,500

Source: U.S. Parks Service

ELLIS ISLAND: THE GOLDEN DOOR, REBURNISHED

Some 100 million Americans either arrived on this shore via Ellis Island or are directly related to those who did. This place, which means so much to so many, was in 1990 reopened to public view after its meticulous (and most expensive, ever, of an American public building) restoration as an architectural and cultural icon and a museum of immigration.

The Great Hall in the main building at Ellis Island.

BIGGEST STATE & COUNTY FAIRS

Fair	Location	Attendance
1. Ohio State Fair	Columbus	3,448,561
2. State Fair of Texas	Dallas	3,411,235
3. State Fair of Oklahoma	Oklahoma City	1,648,928
4. Minnesota State Fair	St. Paul	1,528,688
5. Los Angeles County Fair	Pomona	1,486,343
6. Western Washington Fair	Pullayup	1,343,851
7. Livestock Show & Rodeo	Houston	1,323,865
8. New Mexico State Fair	Albuquerque	1,200,300
9. Tulsa State Fair	Tulsa	1,103,364
10. Del Mar Fair	S. California	1,083,572

MOST POPULAR WATER PARKS

Park	Location	Attendance
1. Wildwater Kingdom	Allentown, PA	921,672
2. White Water	Marietta, GA	800,000
3. Raging Waters	San Dimas, CA	600,000
4. Schlitterbahn Water Park	New Braunfels, TX	500,653
5. Atlantis, The Water Kingdom	Hollywood, FL	465,000
6. Water World	Houston, TX	333,000
7. Water Country USA	Williamsburg, VA	325,551
8. Hyland Hills Water World	Denver, CO	300,000
9. Oceans of Fun	Kansas City, MO	265,371
10. The Beach	Mason, OH	250,000

Source (both charts): Amusement Business Magazine

THE TALLER THE COASTER, THE GREATER THE GATE

Thrill-seekers flock to the tallest/fastest roller coasters, so new ones keep topping old ones (17 opened in '90) as amusement parks fight for the record. A judge ruled that both Dorney Park in Pennsylvania and Six Flags Over Texas had the tallest wooden coaster–depending on how measured. Hang on: in '91, Cedar Point in Ohio opens a new tallest/fastest wooden coaster.

Hercules, "the world's tallest wooden roller coaster," at Dorney Park.

SHOWS

HIGHEST-GROSSING VARIETY/SPECIALTY ACTS

Andrew Dice Clay

Act	Gross Ticket Sales	Attendance	No. of Shows
1. **Andrew Dice Clay** Madison Square Garden, NY, NY	$882,700	35,308	2
2. **The Magic of David Copperfield** Fox Theatre, Detroit, MI	656,160	30,753	9
3. **Penn & Teller** Chicago Theater	396,122	15,417	8
4. **Red Skelton** Fox Theatre, Detroit, MI	372,498	14,055	3
5. **Bill Cosby** Westbury Music Fair, Westbury, NY	351,857	11,001	4
6. **The Magic of David Copperfield** Fox Theatre, Atlanta, GA	325,944	19,062	5
7. **Andrew Dice Clay** Nassau Coliseum Uniondale, NY	321,298	13,000	1
8. **Andrew Dice Clay** Great Western Forum, Inglewood, CA	319,140	14,941	1
9. **Andrew Dice Clay** Palace of Auburn Hills, MI	304,660	15,233	1
10. **Andrew Dice Clay** Palace of Auburn Hills, MI	285,145	11,787	1

Source: Amusement Business Magazine

FORGET THE TAPE MEASURE

It's not a beauty contest anymore, it's "The Miss America Pageant"—"A Scholarship Program." True, the young female entrants still walk around in bathing suits, but that's only so judges can "evaluate a contestant's perseverance and self-discipline in maintaining a physically fit and healthy body." Minds are also taken into account: contestants must write a one-page essay.

Corporate sponsors (including Chevrolet, General Mills, Clairol, Fruit of the Loom) kick in serious money: the 1990 winner, Debbye Turner of Columbia, MO, received $44,000 in scholarships. She earned it: Turner (third African-American to win) spent a year touring 72 cities and 35 states.

The former Miss Missouri.

KIDS' ENTERTAINMENT

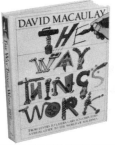

BEST-SELLING CHILDREN'S BOOKS

Title	Author	Publisher	Unit Sales
1. The Way Things Work	David Macaulay	*Houghton Mifflin*	561,452
2. The Great Waldo Search	Martin Handford	*Little, Brown*	304,230
3. Find Waldo Now	Martin Handford	*Little, Brown*	268,706
4. International Children's Bible		*Word*	251,124
5. The Eleventh Hour: A Curious Mystery	Graeme Base	*Abrams*	250,000
6. Swan Lake	Mark Helprin; illus. by Chris Van Allsburg	*Houghton Mifflin*	242,127
7. Macmillan Dictionary for Children		*Macmillan*	195,416
8. Carl Goes Shopping	Alexandra Day	*Farrar, Straus & Giroux*	167,481
9. The Magic Locket	Elizabeth Koda-Callan	*Workman*	161,583
10. The Book of the Sandman	Rien Poortvliet; text by Wil Huygen	*Abrams*	150,000

Source: Publishers Weekly
See note 5, page 90

ALTAR EGOS

Walt Disney Co. sought to acquire Jim Henson Productions in a deal described by Disney CEO Michael Eisner as a "marriage made in children's entertainment heaven." But the near-marriage started breaking up even before the parties reached the altar (though they did effect several joint prenuptial productions). Following the death of namesake and founding genius Jim Henson in May, the negotiations deteriorated into renegotiations. Disney was eager for rights to the Sesame Street characters, which Henson never put on the table, and in the end the price just wasn't right and the deal was annulled. Other suitors are lining up.

KIDS' ENTERTAINMENT

BEST-SELLING TOYS
For December 1990

Product	Company
1. **Nintendo Entertainment System**	Nintendo
2. **Barbie**	Mattel
3. **Super Mario Bros. 3** (game cartridge)	Nintendo
4. **Teenage Mutant Ninja Turtles**	Playmates
5. **Game Boy**	Nintendo
6. **Teenage Mutant Ninja Turtles**	Ultra
7. **Tetris** (game cartridge)	Nintendo
8. **Magic Nursery**	Mattel
9. **My Pretty Ballerina**	Tyco
10. **Go-Go My Walking Pup**	Hasbro

Source: Toy and Hobby World

LARGEST TOY COMPANIES

Company	Sales* ($ millions)
1. Nintendo	$3,200
2. Hasbro	1,460
3. Mattel	1,450
4. Lego	1,000
5. Tonka	775
6. Fisher-Price	600
7. Playmates	470
8. Tyco	450
9. Little Tikes	300
10. Matchbox	200

*Estimates for 1990
Source: Toy and Hobby World research

POWER TURTLES
Hard-Shell Winners

Perennial teenagers, the four Mutant Ninja turtles have been with us (at us?) for seven years, but in 1990 the cartoon/pop phenoms enjoyed their own top-10 grossing movie and a 40-city mock rock concert tour (do turtles have lips?). Now providing spin-off identification to some 600 products, from T-shirts to cookies, they gotta be the reptiles of the decade.

HIGHEST-RATED TELEVISION SERIES

Among children ages 2–11

Series	Network	Rating	Share
1. Bill Cosby Show	NBC	15.3	46
2. A Different World	NBC	15.2	46
3. Simpsons	Fox	14.9	40
4. America's Funniest People	ABC	14.4	44
5. America's Funniest Home Videos	ABC	14.3	42
6. Family Matters	ABC	13.9	39
6. Full House	ABC	13.9	42
8. New Kids on the Block	ABC	12.6	35
9. Perfect Strangers	ABC	12.4	38
9. Roseanne	ABC	12.4	42

Source: Nielsen Media Research

BEST-SELLING KIDS' HOME VIDEOS

1. **Bambi** Walt Disney Home Video
2. **The Land Before Time** MCA/Universal Home Video
3. **Teenage Mutant Ninja Turtles: Killer Pizzas** Family Home Entertainment
4. **Cinderella** Walt Disney Home Video
5. **Charlotte's Web** Paramount Home Video
6. **Teenage Mutant Ninja Turtles: Hot Rodding** Family Home Entertainment
7. **Teenage Mutant Ninja Turtles: The Shredder** Family Home Entertainment
8. **Dumbo** Walt Disney Home Video
9. **Teenage Mutant Ninja Turtles: Heroes** Family Home Entertainment
10. **Winnie the Pooh: New Found Friends** Walt Disney Home Video

Source: BPI Communications, Inc. © 1991.
Used with permission from Billboard

Slimer, star of Real Ghostbusters

CHICKENS AND EGGS

The criticism that Saturday morning TV shows are little more than 30-minute animated ads for toys is not valid...not in 1990. Of the 32 shows offered by the 4 networks, only a few are based on toy properties. A growing number are developed originally for TV—both live action (*Pee Wee's Playhouse*) and animation (*Captain Planet*). The rest have diverse roots: feature films (*Real Ghostbusters*), comic strips (*Garfield*), classic storybooks (*Winnie the Pooh*), music groups (New Kids on the Block), comic celebrities (*Camp Candy*), classic theatrical cartoons (*Bugs Bunny*), and the Muppets (*Muppet Babies*), whatever category that is. Of course, successful shows get turned into toys, so kids have no idea which came first... the TV show (the chicken) or the toy (the egg). But if you try and stop that from happening, the whole American economic system starts to unravel.

CONSUMER PRODUCTS

LARGEST DEPARTMENT & DISCOUNT STORE RETAILERS
Ranked by sales

	Store	Location	Sales ($ millions)
1.	Sears, Roebuck	Chicago, IL	$31,600
2.	K-Mart	Troy, MI	24,210
3.	Wal-Mart	Bentonville, AR	20,970
4.	J.C. Penney	Dallas, TX	14,469
5.	Target	Minneapolis, MI	7,519
6.	Macy's*	New York, NY	6,770
7.	Montgomery Ward	Chicago, IL	5,028
8.	Ames**	Rocky Hill, CT	4,986
9.	Price Club	San Diego, CA	4,901
10.	Sam's	Bentonville, AR	4,841

*Northeast, South and California combined **Filed for bankruptcy in 1990
Source: National Retail Federation (11/90) and Discount Store News (7/90)

LEADING CATALOGS

	Catalog	Buyers/12 mos.
1.	Spiegel	3,800,000
2.	L'eggs	3,700,000
3.	Fingerhut	3,200,000
4.	Lillian Vernon	3,100,000
5.	Avon Fashions	3,000,000
6.	L.L. Bean	1,900,000
7.	Harriet Carter	1,800,000
8.	Miles Kimball	1,700,000
8.	Current	1,700,000
10.	Warshawsky/Whitney	1,600,000

Source: Target Marketing, April 1990

DO THEY SELL CARPETBAGS?

Wal-Mart Stores of Bentonville, AR, now ranks as America's most profitable retailer and could soon rank as America's biggest retailer–despite or maybe due to its preference for small-town (under 25,000 pop.) locations: Wal-Mart's more than 1,500 sell-everything discount stores are dispersed through 28 states. With low prices drawing a low-income clientele, the stores appear to profit at the expense of established local businesses. One recent study suggests that 80% of a typical Wal-Mart's $10-million-a-year business was diverted from existing merchants.

Sam Walton

Source: American Demographics, Wal-Mart Stores, Inc.

BEST-SELLING CARS IN AMERICA

Make/Model	Units Sold
1. Honda Accord	417,179
2. Ford Taurus	313,274
3. Chevrolet Cavalier	295,123
4. Ford Escort	288,727
5. Toyota Camry	284,594
6. Chevrolet Corsica/Beretta*	277,176
7. Toyota Corolla	228,211
8. Honda Civic	220,692
9. Chevrolet Lumina	218,288
10. Ford Tempo	215,290

Source: Motor Vehicle Manufacturers Assn. of the United States, Inc., and Ward's Automotive Reports
*Note: If General Motors reported sales of these models separately–neither would make the top 10. That would make room for the Pontiac Grand Am (also GM) with unit sales of 202,149 in calendar year 1990.

The Japanese have a solid #1 in passenger cars sold in America. The Honda Accord has a 25% lead over its nearest American competitor.

PHOTO: COURTESY HONDA MOTOR CO.

Note: If you include pickup trucks in this list, the Ford F-Series (522,034 units) and the Chevrolet C-Series (487,508) would occupy the top two spots. Take that, Japan!

FROM THE SUBLIME TO THE ELECTRIC

Long the dream of sci-fi writers, over-the-edge environmentalists and shadetree Edisons, the electric-powered car finally attained a measure of realism and respect in 1990 when General Motors announced it is willing and able to mass-produce a battery-powered, pollution-free automobile. The prototype, dubbed Impact (great name for a car; what'll they call the next one, Total?), looks at once sleek and bumptious–in the tradition of other GM "dream" cars. In time, maybe they'll clean up the design along with the atmosphere.

PHOTO: COURTESY OF GENERAL MOTORS

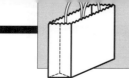

CONSUMER PRODUCTS

LARGEST CONSUMER PRODUCT COMPANIES
Ranked by sales

	Company	Location	Sales ($ millions)
1.	Philip Morris	New York, NY	$39,069
2.	Procter & Gamble	Cincinnati, OH	21,689
3.	PepsiCo	Purchase, NY	15,420
4.	RJR Nabisco	New York, NY	15,224
5.	Sara Lee	Chicago, IL	11,738
6.	Johnson & Johnson	New Brunswick, NJ	9,844
7.	Anheuser Busch	St. Louis, MO	9,481
8.	Coca-Cola	Atlanta, GA	9,171
9.	Borden	New York, NY	7,593
10.	American Brands	Old Greenwich, CT	7,265

Source: Company reports

One product from each of the 10 companies above.

PUT THEM OVER THERE

Among the all-time records set in 1990 was one for new product introductions. Packaged goods in categories such as food products, heath and beauty aids, household supplies, pet products, paper products, and tobacco products, appeared on the nation's retail shelves at a rate over 1,000 new items per month for a total of 13,244. Most were food products, with condiments (2,028 new ones) topping the list. Over 2,300 fresh health and beauty aids hit the market. Among companies, Philip Morris led the way with 278 new food products.

It was probably a good year for manufacturers of shelves.

Source: Gorman's New Product News

LARGEST NEW SHOPPING MALLS
Completed in 1990

Shopping Mall	Location	Square Feet
1. Del Amo Fashion Center	Torrance, CA	3,000,000
2. The Galleria	Houston, TX	2,808,000
3. South Coast Plaza & Town	Costa Mesa, CA	2,600,000
4. Lakewood Center Mall	Lakewood, CA	2,498,000
5. Roosevelt Field Mall	Garden City, NY	2,264,000
6. Sawgrass Mills	Sunrise, FL	2,200,000
7. Randall Park Mall	North Randall, OH	2,097,000
8. Woodfield	Schaumburg, IL	2,000,000
9. Northwest Plaza	St. Ann, MO	1,868,000
10. Franklin Mills	Philadelphia, PA	1,800,000

Source: International Council of Shopping Centers

Del Amo Fashion Center is not only the largest mall completed in 1990, but the largest in the country for the moment.

TOP SPECIALTY RETAIL CHAINS

Chain	Sales ($ millions)
1. Toys "Я" Us	$4,788
2. The Limited	4,648
3. Kinney Shoe	3,042
4. Radio Shack	2,940
5. Circuit City	2,097
6. Marshall's	1,939
7. T.J. Maxx	1,677
8. Gap Inc.	1,587
9. Petrie Stores	1,258
10. US Shoe	1,234

Source: Reprinted by permission, National Retail Federation, Stores magazine, August, 1990.

GOING, GOING, UP!

1990 was a strong year for cashing in on collectibles. Top dollar for an automobile: $2.6 million (before commission) for a 1907 Rolls-Royce Silver Ghost 40/50 hp Tourer, one of only four such cars to survive, from the Rick Carroll collection auctioned by Sotheby's at Palm Beach. Its nearest competitor in 1990 was a 1961 Ferrari 250 GT Berlinetta Competizione, sold for $2.2 million by Christie's at Pebble Beach. The Stratocaster that Jimi Hendrix played at Woodstock was auctioned for $334,620, and an 1830 Shaker work counter went home with Oprah Winfrey for $220,000.

Source: ACS International, "Car Collecting & Investing," Christie's, N.Y. Times, Sotheby's

Jimi Hendrix and his Stratocaster, backstage at Woodstock.

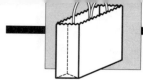

CONSUMER PRODUCTS

LARGEST APPAREL MANUFACTURERS

Company	Sales ($ thousands)
1. Levi Strauss	$3,627,054
2. Sara Lee	2,873,000
3. VF Corp.	2,532,711
4. Liz Claiborne	1,410,677
5. Fruit of the Loom	1,320,900
6. Crystal Brands	857,241
7. Leslie Fay	786,257
8. Kellwood Co.	753,682
9. Russell Corp.	687,954
10. Phillips-Van Heusen Corp.	641,038

Source: American Apparel Manufacturers Assn.

PHOTO: COURTESY OF LEVI STRAUSS & CO.

THE DOLL-RAG BIZ

None of the 20 million or so garments manufactured a year by this company would fit you, unless your name is Tinkerbell, Thumbelina— or Barbie. The name of the company is Mattel and the fashions are designed (about 100 new outfits per annum) for the evergreen Barbie and her statuesque little friends. These are real clothes, designed in southern California and stitched up in real fabric— Mattel estimates that it's used some 75 million yards of cloth since 1959, when they first started draping Barbie—and the sheer numbers place Mattel among America's largest manufacturers of women's clothing.

Sizes run a little small.

EATING & DRINKING

LARGEST FAST-FOOD CHAINS
Ranked by sales

Chain	No. of Outlets	Sales ($ millions)
1. McDonald's	11,162	$17,333
2. Burger King	6,051	5,700
3. Kentucky Fried Chicken	7,945	5,310
4. Pizza Hut	7,410	4,091
5. Wendy's	3,755	3,036
6. Hardee's	3,231	2,921
7. Domino's Pizza	5,220	2,500
8. Dairy Queen	5,206	2,179
9. Taco Bell	3,125	2,130
10. Arby's	2,247	1,300

LEADING TYPES OF RESTAURANTS
From the Restaurant & Institutions 400*

Menu Category	Percent	Sales ($ millions)
1. Hamburgers	31.2%	$31,997
2. Pizza/Italian	10.2	10,519
3. Family dining	8.0	8,209
4. Chicken	7.3	7,472
5. Sweets	5.5	5,679
6. Steak/barbecue	4.9	5,003
7. Dinner houses	4.3	4,443
8. Mexican	3.9	4,028
9. Sandwiches	3.5	3,591
10. Seafood	3.0	3,078

*Menu categories, ranked by sales volume, of the restaurants operated by the 400 largest food service operators.

Source (both charts): Restaurants & Institutions

MCDONALD'S BLOWS OFF FOAM

The world's top fast-food chain didn't grow to well over 11,000 restaurants worldwide by ignoring public wishes. What the world wants now is environmentally sound packaging, so in 1990 McDonald's began phasing out its molded foam sandwich boxes in favor of "alternative packaging options"—presumably something in paper. It's all part of an environmental initiative developed by McD. and the Environmental Defense Fund.

EATING & DRINKING

BEST-SELLING GROCERY STORE ITEMS

Product	Sales ($ millions)
1. Marlboro	$1,509
2. Coke Classic	1,278
3. Pepsi	1,222
4. Kraft Cheese	1,168
5. Diet Coke	996
6. Tide	970
7. Campbell's Soup	964
8. Folger's	824
9. Winston	780
10. Tropicana	685

Source: Information Resources Inc.

RESTAURANTS SERVING THE MOST PEOPLE

Restaurant	Location	Meals Served
1. Hilltop Steak House	Saugus, MA	2,427,600
2. Rascal House	Miami, FL	1,750,000
3. The Omega	Niles, IL	1,543,360
4. Kelly's Roast Beef	Revere, MA	1,152,685
5. Canter's	Los Angeles, CA	1,140,546
6. The Kapok Tree	Clearwater, FL	1,019,397
7. Phillips Harborplace	Baltimore, MD	990,000
7. Zehnder's of Frankenmuth	Frankenmuth, MI	990,000
9. Spenger's Fish Grotto	Berkeley, CA	910,000
10. The Berghoff	Chicago, IL	900,000

Source: Restaurants and Institutions

Chef Jean-Louis Ledent

FIRST A FEW LINES, THEN PÂTÉ

It stands at the intersection of U.S. 45 and Illinois 133, and at the intersection of two improbable interests: bowling and fine French dining. The banner over the maple lanes reads "Welcome to the French Embassy." That's the name of owner/chef Jean-Louis Ledent's combination restaurant and bowling alley in Arcola, IL. Ambitious and successful kitchen favors smoked chops, flambéed kidneys, Coquille St. Jacques, herb cream sauces. Décor: restrained (diners can't hear bowlers). Clientele: tweedy.

MOST POPULAR MIXED DRINKS

Drink	Percent of Orders
1. Tonic (gin and vodka)	23.0%
2. Martini (gin and vodka)	14.0
3. Screwdriver	10.0
4. Bloody Mary	9.0
5. Rum & Cola	7.0
6. Margarita	6.0
6. Bourbon & Cola	6.0
8. Scotch & Soda	5.6
9. 7&7	5.8
10. Bourbon & Water	4.5

Source: Beverage Network, a division of the Beverage Media Group, Ltd., 1990

BEST-SELLING DOMESTIC BEERS

Brand	Barrels (thousands)
1. Budweiser	50,025
2. Miller Lite	19,700
3. Budweiser Light	10,800
4. Coors Light	10,500
5. Busch	9,100
6. Miller High Life	7,500
7. Old Milwaukee	6,950
8. Milwaukee's Best	6,700
9. Coors	5,150
10. Miller Genuine Draft	4,700

Source: Beer Marketer's Insights, Inc.

BREWED BUT UNBOWED

Today's conglomerated megabreweries turn out drinks by and for the mass market—smooth, homogenous and nearly devoid of taste. But America's oldest continuously operating brewery, Yuengling's of Pottsville, PA, produces five idiosyncratic beverages including a brand new Amber Lager, and a dark—nay, opaque—Porter with truly distinct flavor. Yuengling's is still run by the family that started the business in 1829 and still brewed in the same 1831 red-brick mountainside structure, which turns out just 140,000 barrels a year—90% for eastern Pennsylvania only.

CRIME

THE FBI's 10 MOST WANTED FUGITIVES
In alphabetical order

Name/Major Crimes

1. **Armando Garcia**
   Racketeering, narcotics violations (former Miami police officer)
2. **Victor Manuel Gerena**
   Armed robbery
3. **Leo Joseph Koury**
   Racketeering, murder, extortion
4. **Claude Daniel Marks**
   Transportation of illegal firearms and explosives
5. **Melvin Edward Mays**
   Terrorist co-conspirator
6. **Patrick Michael Mitchell** Armed robbery
7. **Leslie Isben Rogge**
   Robbery, wire fraud
8. **Arthur Lee Washington, Jr.**
   Attempted murder (of a NJ state trooper)
9. **Donald Eugene Webb**
   Murder
10. **Donna Jean Willmott**
    Terrorist co-conspirator

Source: Federal Bureau of Investigation

JOINT CHIEFS

Amid the unceasing cries for "more jail time" and "tougher sentencing" that mark America's attitude toward crime, it's worth noting that the U.S. is already the world leader in rate of incarceration. Over a million of our fellow citizens are locked up, which works out to a rate of 426 per 100,000 residents. For black men, the rate is a staggering 3,109 per 100,000— over four times as high as blacks in second-place South Africa. World's third largest jailer of its citizenry is the Soviet Union.

Source: The Sentencing Project, Washington, D.C.

Home for more than a million Americans.

CITIES WITH THE HIGHEST VIOLENT CRIME RATES

1. Miami-Hialeah, FL
2. New York, NY
3. Los Angeles, CA
4. Flint, MI
5. Baltimore, MD
6. Chicago, IL
7. Baton Rouge, LA
8. Jacksonville, FL
9. West Palm Beach-Boca Raton-Delray Beach, FL
10. Memphis, TN

Source: U.S. Department of Justice

More than $500,000 in seized drug money is displayed by Miami law enforcement officials in March of 1990. Two tons of cocaine were also seized.

SAFEST METROPOLITAN AREAS IN AMERICA
or Too Cold for Crooks?

1. Grand Forks, ND
2. Bismarck, ND
3. Sheboygan, WI
4. Fargo-Moorhead, ND–MN
5. Rochester, MN
6. St. Cloud, MN
7. Nashua, NH
8. Binghamton, NY
9. Eau Claire, WI
10. Kokomo, IN

Source: Places Rated Almanac by Richard Boyer and David Savageau, Prentice-Hall, NY

Ice fishing (legal) in Grand Forks, ND.

BLACK DEATH

At the inner-city intersection of drug money and powerful guns, young black males between ages 15 and 24 have been killing each other at such a rate that they are more likely to be murdered than an American soldier was likely to die while serving in Vietnam during that war.

Source: U.S. Centers for Disease Control

A black youth lies dead on the streets of Brooklyn.

TRAVEL

LARGEST AIRLINES

Airline	Total Flight Hours
1. American Airlines	1,181,136
2. Delta Airlines	1,017,937
3. United Airlines	984,422
4. Northwest Airlines	721,517
5. Continental Airlines*	707,953
6. USAir	622,732
7. Trans World Airlines	467,397
8. Eastern Airlines* **	319,480
9. Pan American Airlines*	316,349
10. Southwest Airlines	241,571

*Filed for bankruptcy in 1990. **Ceased operations January 1991.
Source: Federal Aviation Administration

LARGEST HOTEL CHAINS

Ranked by number of rooms

Chain	Rooms
1. Holiday Inn	262,002
2. Best Western	162,887
3. Days Inn	138,611
4. Sheraton	96,456
5. Hilton	96,304
6. Ramada	86,427
7. Marriott	85,199
8. Motel 6	63,341
9. Comfort Inn	62,865
10. Howard Johnson	55,684

Source: Smith Travel Research, provided by the American Hotel/Motel Association

AH SPA!

Two pop-cultural trends of the past decade—narcissism and packaging—have come together in the resort format known as the spa. In one plush location at, say, the Golden Door in Escondido, CA, or the Canyon Ranch in Lenox, MA, "guests" can eat right, exercise every known muscle, attend philosophical/psychological workshops, and have countless sybaritic acts performed on their bodies—including herbal massage, aroma wraps, pedicures, hydrotherapy, and more.

The all-inclusive prices are pegged at a stress-inducing average level of several hundred dollars per night, with the Golden Door peaking at $3,750 for a one-week stay. That works out to $536 per night, but they even furnish the clothes you'll wear all week.

MOST POPULAR DOMESTIC DESTINATIONS FOR FOREIGN TRAVELERS

Destination	No. of Visitors
1. California	7,200,000
2. New York	7,000,000
3. Florida	5,700,000
4. Texas	4,800,000
5. Hawaii	2,800,000
6. Arizona	2,500,000
7. Washington	2,400,000
8. Nevada	1,700,000
9. Michigan	1,600,000
10. Washington, D.C.	1,400,000

Source: U.S. Travel & Tourism Adm., Dept. of Commerce

MOST POPULAR FOREIGN DESTINATIONS FOR AMERICAN TRAVELERS

Destination	No. of Visitors
1. Mexico	14,300,000
2. Canada	12,700,000
3. United Kingdom	2,900,000
4. France	1,900,000
5. Germany	1,800,000
6. Italy	1,200,000
7. Bahamas	1,100,000
8. Japan	921,000
9. Jamaica	751,000
10. Hong Kong	696,000

Source: U.S. Travel & Tourism Adm., Dept. of Commerce

Mayan ruins in Mexico.

THE MOST PUNISHING STRETCHES OF INTERSTATE HIGHWAY IN AMERICA

I-285 in Atlanta, GA
I-90/I-94 in Chicago, IL
I-635 in Dallas, TX
I-610/I-45 in Houston, TX
I-15, I-10, I-110, I-210, I-405, I-605 in Los Angeles, CA
I-95 in Miami, FL
I-95 in New York and New Jersey
I-8 in San Diego, CA
I-80, I-280, I-580, I-880 in San Francisco, CA
I-5 in Seattle, WA

Source: U.S. Dept. of Transportation

COLLEGE

LARGEST UNIVERSITIES

University/State	Student Body
1. **U. of Minnesota,** Minneapolis/St. Paul, Minnesota	61,556
2. **Ohio State U.** (Columbus), Ohio	53,661
3. **U. of Texas** (Austin), Texas	50,106
4. **Michigan State U.,** Michigan	44,480
5. **Miami-Dade Community College,** Florida	43,880
6. **Arizona State U.,** Arizona	43,426
7. **U. of Wisconsin** (Madison), Wisconsin	43,364
8. **Texas A&M U.,** Texas	39,163
9. **U. of Illinois** (Urbana), Illinois	38,337
10. **Pennsylvania State U.** (University Park), Pennsylvania	37,269

Source: National Center for Educational Statistics

MOST EXPENSIVE COLLEGES

Four-year colleges, undergraduate tuition for 1989-90

1. **Bennington College,** Vermont	$16,495
2. **Hampshire College,** Massachusetts	15,070
3. **Bard College,** New York	14,630
4. **Middlebury College,** Vermont	14,610
4. **Wesleyan,** Connecticut	14,610
6. **MIT,** Massachusetts	14,500
7. **Dartmouth College,** New Hampshire	14,465
8. **Princeton U.,** New Jersey	14,390
9. **Swarthmore College,** Pennsylvania	14,380
10. **Johns Hopkins U.,** Maryland	14,360

Source: National Center for Educational Statistics

LARGEST COLLEGE FRATERNITIES

No, fraternities and sororities did not die in the '70s or in the '80s, either. They remain a major factor in social life on college campuses, and despite widespread anti-hazing regulations many continue to threaten the health and well-being of their pledges.

Currently, these are the largest college fraternities by membership:

1. Sigma Alpha Epsilon	214,502
2. Sigma Chi	200,300
3. Lambda Chi Alpha	191,560
4. Phi Delta Theta	176,728
5. Tau Kappa Epsilon	176,072
6. Kappa Sigma	174,387
7. Sigma Phi Epsilon	171,025
8. Sigma Nu	170,000
9. Alpha Tau Omega	152,619
10. Pi Kappa Alpha	152,477

Note: Figures on sorority size and membership are not available, according to the National Panhellenic Council

Source: National Interfraternity Conference, Inc.

MOST POPULAR UNDERGRADUATE DEGREES

Degree	No. Conferred
1. Business (mgmt., office, mktg., dist.)	246,659
2. Social Sciences	107,714
3. Education	96,988
4. Engineering & Engineering Techs.	83,273
5. Health & Health Services	59,111
6. Communications & Comm. Techs.	48,625
7. Psychology	48,516
8. Letters	43,323
9. Visual & Performing Arts	37,781
10. Life Sciences	36,079

Source: National Center for Educational Statistics

MOST POPULAR MASTER'S DEGREES

Degree	No. Conferred
1. Education	82,238
2. Business (mgmt., office., mktg., dist.)	73,154
3. Engineering & Engineering Techs.	24,541
4. Health & Health Services	19,255
5. Public Affairs	17,928
6. Social Sciences	10,854
7. Computer and Information Sciences	9,392
8. Psychology	8,579
9. Visual & Performing Arts	8,234
10. Letters	6,608

Source: National Center for Educational Statistics

ISSUES ON CAMPUS
Hot Topics

When students are not taking in or talking about the items listed herein under "Movies," "Television," "Music," etc., they're likely to focus on racism, classism, sexism, and other real or imagined deviations from "politically correct" thinking in the pages of their texts, the minds of their instructors, or the views of their fellow students.

Among female students, the top issue is date-rape: identifying it, publicizing it, preventing it, and even retaliating for it. At Brown University, women—apparently frustrated by the school's inattention to the problem—took unusually blunt direct action: they began listing the names of alleged student-rapists on campus bathroom walls.

COLLEGE

MOST POPULAR DOCTORAL DEGREES

Degree	No. Conferred
1. Education	6,783
2. Engineering & Engineering Techs.	4,533
3. Physical Sciences & Science Techs.	3,852
4. Life Sciences	3,533
5. Psychology	3,263
6. Social Sciences	2,878
7. Letters	1,238
8. Agriculture and Natural Resources	1,184
9. Theology	1,165
10. Health & Health Services	1,439

Source: National Center for Educational Statistics

LEADING FOREIGN STUDENT ENROLLMENTS

Place of Origin	Total
1. China	33,390
2. Taiwan	30,960
3. Japan	29,840
4. India	26,240
5. Korea	21,710
6. Canada	17,870
7. Malaysia	14,110
8. Hong Kong	11,230
9. Indonesia	9,390
10. Iran	7,440

Source: National Center for Educational Statistics

MBA FEVER

Master of Business Administration programs now rank among the most popular graduate-school choices. About half the MBA degrees ever handed out in America were awarded during the '80s (another symbol of the decade), and the numbers are still rising—about 70,000 graduated this year. No wonder: the average starting salary for an MBA-holder is about $34,000; for graduates of elite business schools like those at Harvard, Northwestern, Stanford, it's in the $60-$70,000 range. And among the CEOs of the top 1,000 U.S. corporations, nearly 25% hold MBAs.

Sources: U.S. Dept. of Education, Business Week's Guide to the Best Business Schools, McGraw-Hill, 1990, The Lindquist-Endicott Report, and research by Catherine Taylor

BEST-SELLING BOOKS ON CAMPUS
Not on the syllabus

Title	Author
1. All I Really Need to Know I Learned in Kindergarten	Robert Fulghum
2. The Calvin and Hobbes Lazy Sunday Book	Bill Watterson
3. The Pre-History of the Far Side	Gary Larson
4. 50 Simple Things You Can Do to Save the Earth	Earthworks Press
5. The Night of the Mary Kay Commandos	Berke Breathed
6. Weirdos from Another Planet!	Bill Watterson
7. Codependent No More	Melody Beattie
8. Foucault's Pendulum	Umberto Eco
9. Clear and Present Danger	Tom Clancy
10. The Cardinal of the Kremlin	Tom Clancy

For the 1989-1990 academic year
Source: Chronicle of Higher Education

INTERCOLLEGIATE CALORIC CHAMPIONS

To study a truly comprehensive offering of snack foods, head for the nearest college-campus store. They've got the cookies, they've got the peanut-butter cups, they've got the popcorn and the chocolate bars. Top seller? Oreos are number one on campus and indeed around the world. Chips Ahoy (chocolate-chip cookies), though, are a close second and may soon take the top spot. Both are Nabisco products.

Source: American Assoc. of College Stores

GOVERNMENT

LARGEST FEDERAL DEPARTMENTS & AGENCIES

Department Agency	Total Employment	1990 Budget* ($ billions)
1. Defense	1,033,730	$328.0
2. Postal Service	816,948	4.1
3. Dept. of Veteran Affairs	248,174	29.9
4. Treasury	158,655	248.5
5. Health and Human Services (including Social Security Admin.)	123,959	519.0
6. Agriculture	122,594	55.1
7. Justice	83,932	8.6
8. Interior	77,681	6.2
9. Commerce	69,920	3.6
10. Transportation	67,364	30.2

* End of fiscal year 1990
Source: U.S. Office of Management and Budget

TOP RECIPIENTS OF U.S. FOREIGN AID

Country	($ millions)
1. Israel	$3,000,000
2. Egypt	2,294,687
3. Pakistan	583,043
4. Turkey	563,750
5. Philippines	494,118
6. El Salvador	382,657
7. Greece	350,700
8. Bangladesh	174,683
9. India	162,802
10. Guatemala	155,751

Source: U.S. Agency for International Development

THROW THE RASCALS IN

1990 was billed as the election year in which incumbents at all levels (local, state and national) would get turned out due to massive voter angst over such gut-felt issues as escalating taxes, evaporating services and epidemic crime plus paralysis over the deficit, defense spending and the steaming S&L mess. Surprise: 96% of incumbent representatives got reelected, and just one senator—Rudy Boschwitz of Minnesota—got sent home. Winning margins were unusually close, though. Tune in again in '92.

BEST-PAID JOBS IN THE FEDERAL GOVERNMENT

Position	Salary
1. President	$200,000 *
2. Vice President	160,600
2. Chief Justice, Supreme Court	160,600
4. Associate Justice, Supreme Court	153,600
5. Department Chairs (Cabinet Secretaries)	138,900
6. Assistant Secretaries, or Heads of Major Bureaus (e.g., Federal Reserve)	125,100
6. House Representatives	125,100
6. U.S. District Court Judge	125,100
9. Deputy Assistant Secretaries, Assistant Heads of Major Bureaus	115,300
10. Heads of Smaller Bureaus (e.g., Fair Housing)	108,300

Note: In case you were wondering, Senators would be #11 at $101,900
* Bush refused his raise
Source: Federal Information Center

WORST ATTENDANCE AT CONGRESSIONAL ROLL CALL VOTES

SENATE

Name	Party/State	Percent of Votes Attended
1. Wilson	R - CA	77 %
2. Armstrong	R - CO	81
3. Hatfield	R - OR	88
4. Wallop	R - WY	91
5. Boren	D - OK	92
6. Boschwitz	R - MN	93
7. Bingaman	D - NM	94
7. Domenici	R - NM	94
7. Johnston	D - LA	94
7. Rudman	R - NH	94

HOUSE

Name	Party/State	Percent of Votes Attended
1. Nelson	D - FL	45 %
2. Crockett	D - MI	48
3. Morrison	D - CT	59
4. Flippo	D - AL	64
4. Ford	D - TN	64
5. Hawkins	D - CA	66
6. Leath	D - TX	70
6. Rowland	R - CT	70
7. Ford	D - MI	75
7. Robinson	D - AK	75

Note: Ties are in alphabetical order   Source (above two charts): The Congressional Record

LARGEST GRANTS GIVEN BY MAJOR AGENCIES

The National Endowment for the Humanities: $1,398,039 to the University of Chicago for preserving and microfilming materials in the UC library.

The National Science Foundation: $17 million+ (in two grants) to Indiana University for its Cyclotron Facility. And, under what the NSF refers to as a "cooperative agreement," over $65 million, went to replace the collapsed radiotelescope at Greenbank, WV.

The National Endowment for the Arts: $1,000,000 (matching grants) to four recipients: Arts and Science Council of Charlotte, NC; San Francisco Symphony Orchestra; Lyric Opera of Chicago; and Arena Stage of Washington, D.C.

DEMOGRAPHICS

LARGEST CITIES

City	Population
1. New York	7,322,564
2. Los Angeles	3,485,398
3. Chicago	2,783,726
4. Houston	1,630,553
5. Philadelphia	1,585,577
6. San Diego	1,110,549
7. Detroit	1,027,974
8. Dallas	1,006,877
9. Phoenix	983,403
10. San Antonio	935,933

Source: 1990 U.S. Census

FASTEST-GROWING METRO AREAS

1980 to 1990

City/State	Percent Growth
1. Moreno Valley, CA	319.6%
2. Rancho Cucamonga, CA	83.5
3. Plano, TX	77.9
4. Irvine, CA	77.6
5. Mesa, AZ	76.1
6. Oceanside, CA	67.4
7. Santa Clarita, CA	65.8
8. Escondido, CA	62.8
9. Arlington, TX	61.7
10. Las Vegas, NV	56.3

Source: U.S. Census Bureau

THE 1990 CENSUS:
Come Out Wherever You Are

New York's Mayor Dinkins

The federal government counted noses again in 1990. Final totals won't be released until 1991, but early results–which showed some big eastern cities losing population (and, therefore, millions in federal aid)–caused gnashing and cries for "recount!" New York mayor David Dinkins dubbed the early numbers "nonsense." As usual, undercounting seems heaviest in black and Hispanic neighborhoods.

Obstacles to an accurate census include deliberate avoidance–a lot of people don't want to be counted. Only 63 percent of the 1990 census forms which were mailed out got returned. A post-census survey will be conducted, to determine just how accurate the 1990 census was.

Metropolitan areas ranked by
EARNINGS PER JOB

Metro Area/State	Average Income
1. New York, NY	$35,751
2. Bridgeport/Stamford/Norwalk/Danbury, CT	33,478
3. San Jose, CA	33,160
4. San Francisco, CA	32,163
5. Anchorage, AK	31,702
6. Middlesex/Somerset/Hunterdon, NJ	31,143
7. Newark, NJ	31,030
8. Bergen-Passaic, NJ	30,703
9. Washington, D.C., MD-VA	29,985
10. Los Angeles/Long Beach, CA	29,841

WEALTHIEST COMMUNITIES
Ranked by income per household

Metro Area/State	Income per Household
1. Bridgeport/Stamford/Norwalk/Danbury, CT	$88,926
2. Lake County, IL	84,721
3. Nassau-Suffolk, NY	81,151
4. Middlesex/Somerset/Hunterdon, NJ	80,476
5. Bergen-Passaic, NJ	76,892
6. Newark, NJ	72,312
7. San Jose, CA	71,812
8. Anaheim/Santa Ana, CA	71,714
9. Anchorage, AK	70,067
10. Trenton, NJ	69,120

Source: (both charts) NPA Data Services, Inc.

WHOOPS!

Into every life a little rain—or other misfortune—must fall. Here, in order of likelihood, are the current bad-news events to beware of.

Happening	Rate per 1,000 Adults
1. Accidental injury, all types	290
2. Accidental injury at home	105
3. Personal theft	85
4. Accidental injury at work	68
5. Injury, motor vehicle accident	23
5. Divorce	23
7. Death, all causes	11
8. Aggravated assault	9
8. Death of spouse	9
10. Robbery	7

Source: Bureau of Justice Statistics, *Report to the Nation on Crime and Justice*

OPINION

BIGGEST BOX-OFFICE BOMBS
*Estimated budgets minus estimated rentals**

Picture	Distributor	Estimated Loss ($ millions)
1. Havana	Universal	$35.0
2. Air America	Tri-Star	25.0
3. Mountains of the Moon	Tri-Star	23.3
4. Two Jakes	Paramount	20.0
4. Stanley & Iris	MGM/UA	20.0
6. Texasville	Columbia	18.5
7. Gremlins II	Warner Bros.	17.0
8. The Desperate Hours	MGM/UA	16.6
9. Bonfire of the Vanities	Warner Bros.	15.0
10. Loose Cannons	Tri-Star	14.0

*Rental income is the studio's take. The split with the theaters varies from picture to picture.
Source: Baseline II Inc.

Charles Keating

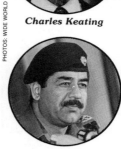
Saddam Hussein

Source: SPY magazine

From the SPY 100
THE MOST APPALLING PEOPLE, PLACES & THINGS OF THE YEAR

1. **S&L Hell**–the greed-induced, corruption-ridden tale of coast-to-coast savings & loan collapses.
2. **Saddam Hussein**–the megalomaniac Iraqi dictator who grabbed Kuwait, threatened practically everybody with apocalyptic warfare, destabilized the Middle East.
3. **Donald Trump**–the very symbol of greed, vulgarity and bluster, parted from his wife, jet, yacht, etc.
4. **Cold Victory**–the end of two generations of the most extensive, most expensive standoff in world history and it was barely noticed.
5. **Racism**–episodes involving blacks, whites, Koreans, Jews showed that this struggle is not over.
6. **First Amendment**–invoked right and left to support or silence public figures from Andy Rooney to Andrew Dice Clay.
7. **George Bush**–the Placebo President. Strategy? Agenda? The man catches fish.
8. **George Steinbrenner**–bad move after bad move finally dropped the once-proud Yankees to the cellar, until baseball finally dropped him.
9. **Hubble Trouble**–blowing $1.5 billion on its flawed telescope, NASA affirmed its status as the gang that couldn't see–or spend–straight.
10. **Cardinal O'Connor**–prelate as publicity hound, floating stories about exorcisms in Queens, about Ivana Trump, and about the eternal future for politicians who support abortion rights.

BLACKWELL'S WORST-DRESSED WOMEN OF THE YEAR

1. **Sinead O'Connor**
   Nothing compares to the bald-headed Banshee of MTV! A New Age Nightmare!
2. **Ivana Trump**
   A Psychedelic Scarecrow! Looks like a cross between Brigitte Bardot — and Lassie!
3. **Glenn Close**
   The Founding Frump of *Nuns Unlimited*! A bad fashion "habit"!
4. **Queen Elizabeth II**
   God Save the Mothballs: The Stonehenge of Style Strikes Again!
5. **Julia Roberts**
   A zoot suit fluke...Godfather III in drag!
6. **Carrie Fisher**
   "Postcards from the Edge"? Sorry, baby, more like Discards from the Dredge!
7. **Kim Basinger**
   Barbie Goes Punk...all Crass...no Class!
8. **Laura Dern**
   A vision of Lust in rags fit for a truck-stop!
9. **Kathy Bates**
   Get the sledgehammer...put this fashion fiasco out of her "Misery"!
10. **Barbra Streisand**
    What can I say? Yentl's gone Mental!

Source: Mr. Blackwell

Sinead O'Connor

THE MOST LIVABLE METROPOLITAN AREAS

1. **Seattle,** WA
2. **San Francisco,** CA
3. **Pittsburgh,** PA
4. **Washington,** DC
5. **San Diego,** CA
6. **Boston,** MA
7. **New York,** NY
8. **Anaheim/Santa Ana,** CA
9. **Louisville,** KY
10. **Nassau/Suffolk Counties,** NY

Source: Places Rated Almanac, by Richard Boyer & David Savageau, Prentice-Hall, NY

OPINION

The Wilderness Society's
10 ENVIRONMENTAL PRIORITIES*

1. Protect ancient forests in the Pacific Northwest
2. Protect the Arctic National Wildlife Refuge
3. End public subsidies for grazing, mining & logging on public land
4. Double the size of the wilderness preservation system
5. Reduce or eliminate development around national parks
6. Restore the Everglades
7. Protect coastal wetland habitats and marine ecosystems
8. Protect the California deserts
9. Protect endangered species
10. Increase protection for national wildlife refuges

National priorities

Defenders of Wildlife
10 OF THE MOST ENDANGERED SPECIES

1. Black-footed ferret
2. California condor
3. Desert tortoise
4. Florida panther
5. Gulf of California porpoise
6. Harpy eagle
7. Kemp's ridley sea turtle
8. Mexican wolf
9. Northern spotted owl
10. Rhinoceros

Mexican wolf

Note: listed in alphabetical order

10 MILESTONES IN THE HISTORY OF POPULAR CULTURE

1. Leif Eriksson discovers America.
Leif's find in the year 1001 sets the stage for the United States, which becomes the world's leading producer and exporter of popular culture (see page 50).

2. The Industrial Revolution.
Economic changes in Britain (c. 1750-1850) beget the concept of leisure time, which begets the concept of finding ways for people to spend their leisure time. With the parallel influx of people into the cities, popular culture becomes dominated by consumerism and mass media.

3. Development of the mail.
In 1477, Louis XI of France pioneers national postal service. This and Gutenberg's printing press are important steps on the ladder to efficient mass communication.

4. The Robin Hood legend begins.
By 1375, Sherwood Forest's favorite son begins to appear in English popular literature. The concept of the outlaw as hero, which will inform so much of Western popular culture, is born.

5. Invention of playing cards.
Building on an earlier Chinese innovation, a Frenchman develops in 1392 the deck that is still in use today from Monte Carlo gambling tables to suburban bridge parties.

6. Mickey Mouse makes his first appearance.
The plucky rodent makes his film debut in the 1928 animated cartoon "Steamboat Willie," and Walt Disney is on his way to developing the world's largest entertainment empire.

7. Daniel Boone, American frontiersman, becomes an international hero.
After publication in 1748 of his so-called autobiography, chock-full of exploits later proven to be false, Boone becomes a trans-Atlantic celebrity. The seeds are planted for the P.T. Barnum theory of popular entertainment: The suckers are out there, if you can come up with a story they'd like to believe.

8. The birth of TV.
In the 1920s Vladimir Zworykin invents his iconoscope, or picture tube, and the first experiments in broadcasting this powerful new medium begin. You know the rest.

9. Shakespeare writes his first plays.
In 1590 or so, the English writer begins producing some respectable literature, demonstrating that the formula of sex, violence and dirty jokes can pack 'em in.

10. The advent of rock & roll.
With Bill Haley's single "Rock Around the Clock" in 1955, rock & roll bursts onto the scene. It turns teens' innate bad attitudes into nothing more threatening than a great mass of potential profits. Elvis Presley, later a bloated cartoon and then a sort of mystical presence at checkout counters, is its most celebrated early practitioner.

Source: Steve Johnson
© Chicago Tribune Company, all rights reserved, used with permission

Robin Hood

NOTES TO THE CHARTS

Note 1 (page 11): **The Billboard charts** are derived from surveys of record store sales activity. Records are ranked according to that analysis. The year-end charts are compiled by computer from Billboard's weekly and biweekly charts during the eligibility period, which is November 18, 1989, through November 17, 1990.

Final year-end chart positioning is based on a point system. Points are given to each record (single or album) for each week on the chart, in a complex inverse relation to the chart position. The point totals are not shown on the charts.

Note 2 (page 20, 22): **The Nielsen television ratings** are derived from monitoring the viewing habits of 4,000 American households. "Rating" numbers represent the estimated percentage of all households with television sets that are tuned to a given show. "Share" numbers represent the estimated percentage of households with television sets <u>in use</u> that are tuned to a given show. Each rating point (for the 1989-1990 season) represents 921,000 households.

Shows are ranked by rating. Share percentages are used to break ties. If both are the same, the shows are ranked as ties.

Note 3 (page 23): The definitions used by Nielsen and the networks to distinguish between "specials," television "movies" and "regularly scheduled programs" can lead to some confusion. For example, the season premiere of a regularly scheduled program, if it's longer than the show's normal length or aired at a time different from the show's normal time period, can be deemed a "special" or a television "movie" - or worse, both. A television "movie" can be defined as a "special" if it is not aired during one of the network's regularly scheduled "movie" time slots (e.g., the ABC Friday Night Movie) and can then be ranked in both categories.

Note 4 (page 44): The Roper Organization's findings on **leisure time interests and hobbies** involved a survey of 2,000 adults.

The complete list from which the "Leisure-Time Pursuits" chart (top) was derived is as follows: Television, Movies, Popular Music, Travel (U.S.), Cooking, Professional Sports, Novels, Non-Fiction Books, Live Theater, Participation Sports, Travel (abroad), Antiques and Collectibles, Rock Music, Detective Fiction, Classical Literature, Romance Books, Symphony, Opera.

The complete list from which the "Hobbies" chart was derived is as follows: Reading, Cooking, Music, Gardening, Pets (cats, dogs, fish, etc.), Fishing, Swimming, Travel, Camping, Crafts (making things), Needlework (knitting, embroidery, etc), Bowling, Sewing, Basketball, Baseball, Golf, Woodworking, Football, Hiking, Photography, Hunting, Tennis, Skiing, Painting (sketching and drawing), Water Sports, Sailing (boating), Hockey.

Note 5 (page 63): The Publishers Weekly chart of best-selling children's books is fundamentally different from the PW charts that appear in our Books section. The Children's Book chart is ranked by actual units sold and not, as with the other charts, based on store surveys of current activity. Since book retailers are permitted to return unsold copies, charts based on actual unit sales take the better part of a year to tabulate. This Children's Books chart, while the most current available, is therefore based on titles released in 1989 and not on the 1990 releases that are the subject of the Publishers Weekly adult book charts (see pages 25-27).

ANY SUGGESTIONS?

We'd love to hear from you. Since this book is an annual event, we have the opportunity to respond to our readers in a very specific way. We'd like your reaction to this year's presentation and your ideas for next year's. We want to improve and expand each edition.

T-Shirt Offer!

If you send us an idea for a new chart that we use in next year's edition, we'll send you a Top 10 T-Shirt (X-large only). The chart must be factual and verifiable from a source that is authoritative and respected and one that will grant us permission to publish the information in our format.

Address correspondence to: Top 10 Almanac, Workman Publishing Co., 708 Broadway, New York, NY 10003

INDEX

Abyss, The, 19
Academy Awards, 18-19
Actors and actresses, highest-paid, 17
Advances, in book publishing, 27
Advertising, 53-55
    biggest-spending national advertisers, 53
    on Channel One, 55
    largest agencies, 54
    leading media companies, 55
    magazines with highest revenue from, 29
    national ad spending ranked by category, 53
    national ad spending ranked by media, 55
    in Saturday morning TV shows, 65
    top mega-brand advertisers, 54
    truth in, 54
Age-Old Friends, 21
Air Force, U.S., 56
Airlines, largest, 76
Alydar, 41
America, discovery of, 89
American Playhouse, 21
Amusement parks:
    most popular, 58
    tallest and fastest roller coasters at, 61
"Andre's Mother," 21
Apparel manufacturers, largest, 70
Aquariums, most popular, 59
Archer, Jeffrey, 27
Arena Stage, 83
Arts and Science Council of Charlotte, N.C. 83
Ashman, Howard, 19
As Nasty as They Wanna Be, 12
Associated Universities, Inc., 83
Athletes, highest-paid, 40
Attractions, 58-61
    biggest state and county fairs, 61
    Ellis Island, 60
    most popular aquariums, 59
    most popular national parks, 60
    most popular theme and amusement parks, 58
    most popular water parks, 61
    most popular zoos, 59
    roller coasters, 61
    Universal Studios Florida, 58
Aura, 15
Automobiles. *See* Cars
Auto racing, top money winners in, 41
Awards:
    Academy, 18-19
    Emmy, 20-21
    Grammy, 11, 14-15
    Tony, 34, 35

Baker, Anita, 15
Banking crisis, 48
Barbie (doll), 70
Barnum, P.T., 89
Barr, Roseanne, 40
Barrie, Dennis, 59
Bartok: Six String Quartets, 15
Baseball:
    Barr's national anthem performance, 40
    batting averages, 43
    earned run averages, 43
    Rose's conviction, 42
    Steinbrenner's ouster, 42
    surprises in 1990 season, 39
    World Series, 38, 39
Basketball:
    1990 champions, 38
    rebounding averages, 43
    scoring averages, 43
    top-ranked college teams, 42
Batman, 19
Batting averages, 43
Beauty contests, 62
Beers, best-selling domestic, 73
Bel-Air Hotel (Los Angeles), 76
Belmont Park, 41
Bergen, Candice, 20
Billionaires, American, 47
Black enterprises, largest, 48
Black men:
    drug-related murders among, 75
    incarceration rate for, 74
Blackwell's worst-dressed women of 1990, 87
Blockbuster Entertainment Corp., 36
Bolton, Michael, 14
Books, 25-27, 50
    advances paid for, 27
    for children, best-selling, 63
    on college campuses, best-selling, 81
    hardcover fiction best-sellers, 25
    hardcover nonfiction best-sellers, 26
    Ivana Trump's deal, 25
    largest publishers, 25
    mass-market paperback best-sellers, 27
    Random House editorship, 26
    trade paperback best-sellers, 27
Boone, Daniel, 89
Born on the Fourth of July, 18, 19
Boschwitz, Rudy, 82
Boston Bruins, 38
Boston *Herald,* 43
Bowling, top money winners in, 41
Boycott of Nike sneakers, 53
Breeders' Cup, 41
Brenner, David, 19
Brewery, oldest continuously operating, 73
Bride's, 31
Broadway:
    all-time longest-running show on, 35
    longest-running current shows on, 35
    top-grossing shows on, 34
Brown, Bobby, 15
Brown, Tina, 26
Bruno, John, 19
Brush, Bob, 21
B-2 bomber, 56
Bugs Bunny, 65
Bush, George, 40
Bush, Neil, 48
Business, 46-52
    American billionaires, 47
    best-performing stocks, 52
    biggest deals, 52
    economic indicators, 51
    entertainment media, 50
    fastest-growing small private companies, 48

highest-paid chief executives, 49
highest-paid entertainers, 17, 46
insider-trading scandals, 52
Japanese acquisition of U.S. companies, 47
largest black enterprises, 48
largest industries, 50
largest junk bond defaults, 47
largest U.S. exporters, 50
largest U.S. industrial corporations, 46
largest U.S. service corporations, 46
MBAs in, 80
most valuable corporations, 49
return on investments, 51
savings & loan crisis, 48
Trump's fall, 49
See also Advertising; Consumer products; Technology

Cable television:
　leading networks, 21
Campbell, Luther, 12
Camp Candy, 65
Cannon, 17
Captain Planet, 65
"Caroline?", 20, 21
Carroll, Rick, 69
Cars:
　auction prices for, 69
　best-selling, 67
　electric-powered, 67
　misleading advertising for, 54
Carter, Thomas, 21
Catalogs, leading, 66
Cedar Point, 61
Censorship, 12
Census, 84
Channel One, 55
Cheers, 20
Chick Corea Akoustic Band, 15
Chief executives:
　highest-paid, 49
　MBAs among, 80
Chips Ahoy, 81
Chorus Line, A, 35
Christie's, 69
Cincinnati Reds, 38, 39, 40
Cinema Paradiso, 19
Cities and metropolitan areas:
　fastest-growing, 84
　with highest violent crime rates, 75
　largest, 84
　most livable, 87
　ranked by earnings per job, 85
　safest, 75
　wealthiest, 85
City of Angels, 34
Clancy, Tom, 27
Classical albums, best-selling, 15
Classism, as issue on college campuses, 79
Clothes:
　Blackwell's worst-dressed women, 87
　for dolls, 70
　largest apparel manufacturers, 70
Collectibles, auction prices for, 69
College, 78-81
　best-selling books not on syllabus, 81
　favorite snack foods at, 81
　hot issues at, 79
　largest fraternities, 78
　largest universities, 78

　leading foreign student enrollments, 80
　MBA degrees, 80
　most expensive, 78
　most popular doctoral degrees, 80
　most popular master's degrees, 79
　most popular undergraduate degrees, 79
　top-ranked basketball teams, 42
　top-ranked football teams, 42
Columbia Pictures, 47
Columbo, 21
Comics, 32
Computers, personal, 57
Concert tours, top-grossing, 14
Condé Nast Traveler, 26
Congress, U.S., 48, 84
　worst attendance at roll call votes in, 83
Consumer Price Index (CPI), 51
Consumer products, 66-70
　best-selling cars in America, 67
　collectibles, auction prices for, 69
　doll clothes, 70
　largest consumer product companies, 68
　largest department and discount store retailers, 66
　largest new shopping malls, 69
　leading catalogs, 66
　most profitable retailer of, 66
　new, introduced in 1990, 68
　top specialty retail chains, 69
Contemporary Arts Center (Cincinnati), 59
Corporations:
　largest, 46
　most valuable, 49
Country albums, best-selling, 13
County fairs, biggest, 61
Crime, 74-75
　drug-related murders, 75
　FBI's 10 most wanted fugitives, 74
　incarceration rate, 74
　safest metropolitan areas in America, 75
　sneaker/violence linkup, 53
　violent, cities with highest rates of, 75
Cronyn, Hume, 21
Cult video stores, 37

Daly, Tyne, 34
Danson, Ted, 20
Date-rape, 79
Davis, Miles, 15
Daytime drama, 23
Dead Poets Society, 19
Defense Department, U.S., 56
Dell, 27
Demographics, 84-85
　bad-news events, 85
　earnings per job, 85
　fastest-growing metro areas, 84
　largest cities, 84
　1990 census, 84
　wealthiest communities, 85
Denver Broncos, 38
Detroit Pistons, 38
Dinkins, David, 84
Dinner, Michael, 21
Doctoral degrees, most popular, 80
Doll clothes, 70
"Don't Know Much," 14
Dorney Park, 61
Dow Jones, 51
Drexel Burnham Lambert, 52

Driving Miss Daisy, 18
Drugs, murders related to, 75
Drug Wars: The Camarena Story, 20

Earned run averages, 43
Earnings per job, metropolitan areas ranked by, 85
Eating and drinking, 71-73
   best-selling domestic beers, 73
   best-selling grocery store items, 72
   on college campuses, 81
   environmentally sound packaging, 71
   French restaurant/bowling alley, 72
   largest fast-food chains, 71
   leading types of restaurants, 71
   most popular mixed drinks, 73
   oldest continuously operating brewery, 73
   restaurants serving most people, 72
Economic indicators, 51
Edmonton Oilers, 38
Egg, 28, 29
Elections, 82
Electric-powered car, 67
Electronics, home, 56
Ellis Island, 60
Emerson String Quartet, 15
Emmy Awards, 20-21
Endangered species, 88
End of the Innocence, The, 15
Entertainers, highest-paid, 17, 46
Entertainment media:
   export of, 50
   See also Books; Kids' entertainment; Magazines; Movies; Music; Radio; Television; Theater
Entertainment Weekly, 28, 29
Environmental Defense Fund, 71
Environmental priorities, 88
Equal Justice: Promises to Keep, 21
Eriksson, Leif, 89
E.T., 47
Evans, Harry, 26
Evans, Joni, 26
"Every Little Step," 15
Exercise, most efficient forms of, 45
Exotic dance industry, trade magazine for, 30
Exporters, largest U.S., 50

Falk, Peter, 21
Fast-food chains:
   largest, 71
   packaging used by, 71
FBI's 10 most wanted fugitives, 74
Ferrari 250 GT Berlinetta Competizione, 69
Fiction best-sellers, 25
Fisher, Jules, 34
Follett, Ken, 27
Football:
   1990 champions, 38
   quarterback efficiency, 43
   top-ranked college teams, 42
   total yards rushing, 43
   women reporters in locker rooms, 43
Forbes, 29
Foreign aid, top recipients of, 82
Foreign films, top-grossing, 18
Foreign student enrollments, 80
Francis, Freddie, 19
Fraternities, largest, 78

French Embassy (Arcola, Il.), 72
Furst, Anton, 19

Galati, Frank, 34
Gambling, most popular forms of, 45
Garfield, 65
Geffen Records, 47
General Hospital, 23
General Motors, 67
"Girl You Know It's True," 11
Giving You the Best That I Got, 15
Glory, 18, 19
Go For Wand, 41
Golden Door, 76
Golf, top money winners in, 41
Golson, Barry, 28
Government, 82-83
   federal, best-paid jobs in, 83
   federal, largest departments and agencies in, 82
   largest grants given by major agencies, 83
   1990 census, 84
   1990 elections, 82
   top recipients of U.S. foreign aid, 82
   worst attendance at congressional roll call votes, 83
Grammy Awards, 11, 14-15
Grand Hotel, 34
Grants, largest given by major agencies, 83
Grapes of Wrath, The, 34
Grocery store items, best-selling, 72
Gypsy, 34

Haley, Bill, 89
Hallmark Hall of Fame, 20, 21
Hammer, M.C. (né Stanley Burrell), 13
HarperCollins, 27
Harvard Business School, 80
Hendrix, Jimi, 69
Henley, Don, 15
Jim Henson Productions, 63
Hershey, Barbara, 21
Hobbies, most-preferred, 44
Hockey, 1990 champions in, 38
Home videos, 36-37, 50
   best-selling, 37
   best-selling music videos, 14
   best-selling non-motion picture, 37
   cult stores, 37
   for kids, best-selling, 65
   rental/sales megabusiness, 36
   top rentals, 36
Horse racing:
   top money winners in, 41
   tragedies in, 41
Hotels:
   largest chains, 76
   most expensive, 76
"How Am I Supposed to Live Without You?", 14
Hubble Space Telescope, 57
Hutshing, Joe, 19

Impact, (car), 67
Incarceration, rate of, 74
Incumbents, reelection of, 82
Indiana University, 83
Industrial Revolution, 89
Industries, largest, 50
Insider-trading scandals, 52
Interstate highway, most punishing

stretches of, 77
Investments, return on, 51

Jackson, Jesse, 53
Japan, U.S. companies sold to businesses based in, 47
Jaws, 47
Jazz albums, best-selling, 13
Jobs:
    best-paid in federal government, 83
    earnings per, metropolitan areas ranked by, 85
Junk bonds:
    insider-trading scandals in, 52
    largest defaults of, 47

Keating, Charles, 48
Keiley, David, 21
Kerkorian, Kirk, 17
Kiam, Victor, 43
Kids' entertainment, 63-65
    best-selling books, 63
    best-selling home videos, 65
    best-selling toys, 64
    Disney/Henson deal, 63
    highest-rated television series, 65
    largest toy companies, 64
    Teenage Mutant Ninja Turtles, 64
Killing in a Small Town, A, 21

L.A. Law, 20, 21
Ledent, Jean-Louis, 72
Leisure time, 44-45
    Monopoly, 45
    most efficient forms of exercise, 45
    most popular forms of gambling, 45
    most-preferred leisure-time interests, 44
    origin of concept, 89
    television watching, 44
Lettice and Lovage, 34
Lewis, Daniel Day, 18
Lincoln Savings and Loan, 48
Little Mermaid, The, 19
Loquasto, Santo, 34
Louis XI, King of France, 89
Lynch, David, 24
Lynn, Amber, 30
Lyric Opera of Chicago, 83

McDonald's, 71
McNally, Terrence, 21
Magazines, 28-31
    heaviest, 31
    with higest advertising revenue, 29
    with highest paid circulation, 28
    largest publishing companies, 31
    most profitable for retailers, 30
    1990 startups, 28-30
Mail, development of, 89
Mapplethorpe, Robert, 59
Master of Business Administration (MBA), 80
Master's degrees, most popular, 79
Matsushita Electrical Industrial Co., 47
Mattel, 70
MCA, 47
Media companies, leading, 55
Menken, Alan, 19
Men's Life, 28
Metropolitan areas. *See* Cities and metropolitan areas

MGM/UA, 17
Mickey Mouse, first appearance of, 89
Midler, Bette, 14
Milken, Michael, 52
Milli Vanilli, 11
Miss America Pageant, 62
Mr. Nickerson, 41
Mixed drinks, most popular, 73
Monopoly, 45
Morning Drive, 33
William Morris Agency, 25
Morse, Robert, 34
Morvan, Fabrice, 11
Movies, 16-19, 50
    Academy Awards, 18-19
    biggest box-office bombs, 86
    highest-budgeted, 18
    highest-paid actors and actresses, 17
    leading independent film companies, 19
    MGM/UA sale, 17
    Mickey Mouse's debut in, 89
    studios ranked by market share, 17
    studios sold to Japanese, 47
    television, highest-rated, 23
    top-grossing feature films, 16
    top-grossing foreign films in America, 18
    top-grossing independently produced feature films, 19
Mowatt, Zeke, 43
Muppet Babies, 65
Muppets, 63
Murders, drug-related, 75
Murdoch, Rupert, 26
Murdoch Magazines, 28
Muren, Dennis, 19
Murphy Brown, 20
Music, 11-15, 50
    advent of rock & roll, 89
    best-selling classical albums, 15
    best-selling country albums, 13
    best-selling jazz albums, 13
    best-selling music videos, 14
    best-selling pop albums, 11
    best-selling rap singles, 12
    best-selling rhythm & blues albums, 12
    censorship of, 12
    Grammy Awards, 14-15
    Milli Vanilli controversy, 11
    rap, 12, 13
    top-grossing concert tours, 14
    top pop artists, 15
My Left Foot, 18

Nabisco, 81
NASA, 57
National anthem, Barr's performance of, 40
National Basketball Association, 38
National Endowment for the Arts, 59, 83
National Endowment for the Humanities, 83
National Football League, 38
National Hockey League, 38
National parks, most popular, 60
National Science Foundation, 83
Naughton, James, 34
Neville, Aaron, 14
New England Patriots, 43
Newhouse, S.I., 26
New Kids on the Block, 65
New product introductions, 68
Newspapers:
    Largest dailies, 32

New York *Daily News* strike, 32
New York Yankees, 42
Nick of Time, 14
Nike Air Jordans, 53
No-hitters, 39
Nonfiction best-sellers, 26
Northern Dancer, 41
Northop, 56
Northwestern Business School, 80

Oakland Athletics, 38, 39
Obscenity charges:
    Mapplethorpe exhibit and, 59
    rap music and, 12
Ol' Claude, 33
Olson, Lisa, 43
Operation PUSH, 53
Opinion, 86-88
    biggest box-office bombs, 86
    Blackwell's worst-dressed women, 87
    most appalling people, places and
      things of year, 86
    most endangered species, 88
    most livable metropolitan areas, 87
    most significant milestones in the
      history of popular culture, 89
    top environmental priorities, 88
Oreos, 81

Packaging, environmentally sound, 71
Panasonic, 47
Paperback best-sellers, 27
Parretti, Giancarlo, 17
Pathé Communications, 17
Pay television, 50
Pee Wee's Playhouse, 65
People, 29
Perkin-Elmer Corporation, 57
Personal computers, 57
Philip Morris, 68
Photography, obscenity controversy and, 59
Pilatus, Rob, 11
Piniella, Lou, 39
Playing cards, invention of, 89
Please Hammer Don't Hurt 'Em, 13
Pop albums, best-selling, 11
Pop artists, top, 15
Portland Trailblazers, 38
Postal service, 89
Presley, Elvis, 89
Printing press, 89

Quarterback efficiency, 43
Quasar, 47

Racehorses. *See* Horse racing
Racism, as issue on college campuses, 79
Radio:
    leading stations, 33
    most popular National Public Radio
      programs, 33
    Tomlinson's personalities, 33
    Top formats, 33
Radiotelescopes, 83
Raitt, Bonnie, 14
Random House, 25, 26
Rap music, 12, 13
Real Ghostbusters, 65
Rebounding averages, 43
Recording business, 50
Reebok Pumps, 53

Restaurants:
    fast-food, packaging at, 71
    French, bowling alley combined
      with, 72
    largest fast-food chains, 71
    serving most people, 72
Retailers:
    largest, 66
    most profitable, 66
    most profitable magazines for, 30
    top specialty chains, 69
Rhythm & blues albums, best-selling, 12
Robin Hood legend, 89
Rock & roll, advent of, 89
"Rock Around the Clock," 89
Roller coasters, 61
Rolls-Royce Silver Ghost Tourer, 69
Ronstadt, Linda, 14
Rose, Pete, 42

San Diego Padres, 40
San Francisco 49ers, 38
San Francisco Symphony Orchestra, 83
Sargent, Joseph, 21
Saturday morning TV shows, 65
Savings & loan crisis, 48
Scali, McCabe, Sloves Inc., 54
Schulman, Tom, 19
Scoring averages (basketball), 43
Senate, U.S., 48
Sentencing, for crimes, 74
Sexism, as issue on college campuses, 79
Shaker Knit, 41
Shakespeare, William, 89
Shopping malls, largest new, 69
Shows:
    highest-grossing variety/specialty acts, 62
    Miss America Pageant, 62
Silverado Savings, 48
Six Flags Over Texas, 61
Skotak, Dennis, 19
Smith, Maggie, 34
Snack foods, most popular on college
    campuses, 81
Sneakers, 53
Soap operas, 23, 24
Sony, 47
Sotheby's, 69
South Africa, 74
Soviet Union, 74
Spas, prices at, 76
Spira, Howie, 42
Sports, 38-43, 50
    highest-paid athletes, 40
    most-watched sporting events, 39
    1990 winners, 38
    participation, most popular, 39
    spectator, most popular, 38
    top money winners, 41
    women reporters in locker rooms, 43
    See also Baseball; Basketball; Football;
      Horse racing
Stanford Business School, 80
"Star-Spangled Banner," 40
State fairs, biggest, 61
Steinbrenner, George, 39, 42
Stocks, best-performing, 52
Stone, Oliver, 18
Stratocaster, 69
Strike at New York *Daily News,* 32
Surviving at the Top (Trump), 25, 49

Taj Mahal (Atlantic City, N.J.), 49
Tandy, Jessica, 18
Tanii, Akio, 47
Technics, 47
Technology, 56-57
    best-selling home electronics, 56
    best-selling personal computers, 57
    best-selling personal computer software, 57
    B-2 bomber, 56
    Hubble Space Telescope, 57
    largest high-technology companies, 56
Teenage Mutant Ninja Turtles, 64
Telescope, space, 57
Television, 20-24, 50
    birth of, 89
    Channel One, 55
    Emmy Awards, 20-21
    General Hospital, 23
    highest-rated movies, 23
    highest-rated network series, 20
    highest-rated new shows, 22
    highest-rated public television
        programs, specials or limited series, 24
    highest-rated public television series,
        regularly scheduled, 24
    highest-rated series, among children, 65
    highest-rated shows of all time, 22
    highest-rated specials, 23
    highest-rated syndicated series, 21
    leading cable networks, 21
    most prolific producers of primetime
        network shows, 22
    most-watched sporting events on, 39
    Saturday morning shows, 65
    time spent watching, 44
    Twin Peaks, 24
Tennis, top money winners in, 41
Theater, 34-35
    all-time longest-running Broadway show, 35
    longest-running current Broadway
        shows, 35
    Shakespeare's first plays, 89
    Tony Awards, 34, 35
    top-grossing Broadway shows, 34
Theme parks, most popular, 58
thirtysomething, 20
Time, Inc., 50
Time magazine, 50
Tomlinson, Claude, 33
Tony Awards, 34, 35
Toys, 64
    Saturday morning TV shows and , 65
Travel, 76-77
    largest airlines, 76
    largest hotel chains, 76
    most expensive hotels, 76
    most popular domestic destinations for
        foreign travelers, 77
    most popular foreign destinations for
        American travelers, 77
    most punishing stretches of interstate
        highway, 77
Traveling Wilburys, 14
Treasury bills, 51
Tru, 34
Trump, Donald, 25, 49
Trump, Ivana, 25, 49
Turner, Debbye, 62

Twin Peaks, 24
2 Live Crew, 12

"U Can't Touch This," 13
Undergraduate degrees, most popular, 79
"Under the Sea, " 19
Unemployment, 51
Universal Pictures, 47
Universal Studios Florida, 58
University of Chicago, 83
U.S. Hot Rod Association, 54
U.S. Stripper, 30

Vanity Fair, 26
Variety/specialty acts, highest-grossing, 62
Videos. *See* Home videos
Vietnam War, 75
Volvo, 54

Wagner, Robin, 34
Wall Street insider-trading scandals, 52
Wal-Mart stores, 66
Walt Disney Co., 63, 89
Walt Disney World, 58
Washington, Denzel, 18
Water parks, most popular, 61
Wealthiest communities, 85
Wettig, Patricia, 20
Whittle Communications, 85
"Wind Beneath My Wings," 14
Winfrey, Oprah, 69
Winnie the Pooh, 65
WIVK-AM (Knoxville, Tenn.), 33
Women sports reporters, 43
Wonder Years, The, 21
Wood, Kimba, 52
Woodstock, 69
World Series, 38, 39

Yards rushing (football), 43
Yeatman, Hoyt, 19
Yeungling's, 73
Young, Peter, 19

Zoos, most popular, 59
Zworykin, Vladimir, 89